**OVERCOME DOUBT AND UNDERSTAND
HOW FAITH REALLY WORKS**

MORE

ANDY THOMPSON

Dedication

To Kenneth E. Hagin, who taught me Faith.

To Lashawn, Alexandra, Kayla, Kerwin, Robert, and AJ for teaching me Love.

Table of Contents

Introduction

Mark 11:23 (NKJV)

23 "For assuredly, I say to you, whoever says to this mountain, 'Be removed and be cast into the sea,' and does not doubt in his heart, but believes that those things he says will be done, he will have whatever he says."

What does it actually mean to move a Mountain? Have you ever really considered that? I was recently in Denver Colorado and had the opportunity to actually stand at the foot of a mountain. Not a hill, not a mound of dirt, but an actual mountain that had been there before I was born and will be there after we are all long gone. That's when the sheer weight of what Jesus said in Mark 11, really hit me.

I can only assume that many of you, like me, have seen this passage before; you have heard it preached and explained. However, I do have to realize that for many, Mark 11:23 is brand new. If that is the case, let's address you all first. You NEWBIES!

If Mark 11:23 is a new revelation, that is a wonderful thing. This book will be a real blessing in your life. You are about to unlock a secret power, a strength that God has kept set apart for us, for the glory of His children. That secret power is FAITH. And FAITH is the key to the impossible!

Now, just so that we all start out on the same page, let me really quickly define the term FAITH. When I say Faith I mean... **A confidence that something, someone, or some outcome, that is still unseen will absolutely happen.**

This FAITH, this confidence, has a direct effect on your behavior in 3 major ways:

1. You do not allow feelings to rule you.
2. You have courage and boldness since anything is possible!
3. You learn to let go and trust God.

If you are new to faith, that is a good place to begin, and we will explain more as we go, but that is a good start.

Now...

For the rest of us, those who have read this passage, heard it taught and considered it seriously, I have a different recommendation. Perhaps it may even be seen as a bit of a warning. Those of us familiar with scripture have to be careful that we do not lose the ability to continually get revelation. In other words, the minute you think you have the WORD figured out, that is the exact moment that it can surprise you, and hopefully, bless you in a whole new way if you are determined to stay open.

I have been there. I attended Rhema Bible Training Center in the 80's. I sat in class with Brother Hagin, so I thought I had heard all the messages on faith! Or had I? Actually, I started reading Mark 11 in light of my current circumstances and I have seen Mountain Moving in a whole new light.

It reminds me of something that Brother Hagin said to us in a class. I trust that you are ok with me quoting Kenneth Hagin, since in my estimation he is one of the modern day fathers of faith. He said to us in a class, something to the effect of...

"Great Faith does not come from books; great faith comes as a result of great trial."

I was 18 at the time, so my immediate response in my head was, "well then why am I reading your book?" Of course I only thought that, I didn't say it out loud. Someone may have yelled, "BLASPHEMY!" But his statement baffled me. I was at Rhema; I went there from Boston right out of High School. I had opportunities to attend Ivy League schools and I had spurned that to move to Tulsa, to attend a Bible Training Center. My guidance counselor thought I was out of my mind. I had made this sacrifice and now it sounded like he was telling us we had wasted our time.

Of course, that was not his point. I couldn't see that then, I was only 18. But today, over 20 years later, I realize what he meant. He wasn't saying that reading and studying was a waste, he was simply stating a fact that was not so obvious to me at the time, but is glaringly obvious to me now. And that statement is:

Reading and learning is nothing in comparison to walking.

You think you know something, until you experience it. You think you know about babies, until you are on the table pushing one out, until your hand is being squeezed and broken by a woman as she bears down to push out your child. You think you know about being grown, until you move out of your parent's house. You can read about running a company, but that is nothing in comparison to actually becoming CEO. You can study the dynamics of a roller coaster, but until you are strapped in, going up that first drop, wondering how you let your teenagers talk you into getting on this ride, wondering, "what was I thinking?" Until you are there, you know nothing about roller coasters.

Today – faith means something totally different to me. Today, much like when I stood at the foot of that mountain, I realize that I used to think I knew faith, but I was wrong.

I KNOW I am not alone. You thought you knew God, until these mountains popped up. And today, after the recent economic crash, after the attack against the country, after the instability of the governmental system, after what you have been through with your family, after your diagnosis, after your divorce, after what you went through with your daughter, after you got custody of your grandchildren and after LIFE LET YOU DOWN, you now realized that this is a war and that Paul was right, you have to put on armor every day because the devil means business! After all of that, now, like me, you are looking at Mountains, and Mountain Moving in a whole new light.

You realize that what you heard before was more than just church jargon to get you to say "amen." This thing is real! That is what is in your mind right now! This thing is REAL, this attack is Real, and I am going to have to get ready if I am going to have what God has for me.

I KNOW I AM NOT ALONE! I can hear you all saying, "Amen."

The Spirit warned us, that we would have to fight the good fight of the faith. He warned us that we would have to fight to take hold of that for which Christ took hold of us. We should not be surprised at the painful trials we are enduring, as though something strange was happening to us. This is a battle, this is more than church, this is real life.

If that resonates with you, then I have hope for you. This book has a word for you. Understand, mountains can be moved, your mountain will be moved, and I am here to help you move it. And actually, I would contend that the mountain is a path to greatness. I would contend that there is no success without mountains. When you want more, mountains will be a part of the landscape. So, since you should want more, expect mountains.

It begins with BELIEF. It is so interesting, but it takes Faith even to read a book on Faith. You have to first believe that it is possible to get more. I am here to express to you that what Jesus said is true: "with man, things are impossible, but not with God, ALL things are possible if you can simply believe."

I want you to believe again. I want you to chase more and refuse to be intimidated by the mountains that accompany the more. Decide right now, I can be healed, I can be free, I can lose weight, I can get my degree, I can overcome my fear, I can save my marriage, I can reach MORE, I can, I can, I can!

I can do ALL things through Christ who gives me the strength. I can even scale the mountain!

So let's get to it! I suggest you grab a notebook and a pen, so that you can jot down the steps we give you. For many of you, like me, this is serious. You have something that only God can do for you. I have some things that only God can do for me. If God does not do it, it will not get done. But I am glad that power is available to me.

That is the ultimate lesson of Mark 11. You can bless and you can curse. Let's get after the blessing, let's start the fight and grab the life that God intended for us. It IS POSSIBLE, what you wish for IS POSSIBLE, your healing IS POSSIBLE, your new career IS POSSIBLE, the scholarship IS POSSIBLE. ANYTHING IS POSSIBLE if you can only BELIEVE!

Chapter 1

MOUNTAIN MOVERS

Mark 11:22-23

22 "Have faith in God," Jesus answered. 23 "Truly I tell you, if anyone says to this mountain, 'Go, throw yourself into the sea,' and does not doubt in their heart but believes that what they say will happen, it will be done for them.

I don't want to make you wait another minute. You picked up a book that is titled, "More," so let's jump right in and break it down. The most important word for us to focus on is the word: **MORE**.

I know that your eye wants to focus on the word **Mountain**, and believe me, we are going to focus on the mountains that we all have to face.

But here in the beginning, I want us to get something straight. Understand that when we start to talk about moving a mountain, what we are really talking about is getting from here to there. What we are really talking about is getting you to your ultimate place in God. Ultimately, every believer finds themselves on a journey. Although we are talking about moving the mountain, the real question is...

How Do I Get from Here to There?

How do I get to the place of destiny that God has for me?

You see, Mark 11:23 is a word for **MOVERS**! And when you think of yourself as a **MOVER**, don't just think about the mountain being moved. I want you to think about yourself being moved.

I started on this search for faith looking for power. I knew that I was called and I knew that God wanted me to help people. But I was also fascinated by the idea of having power. However, I soon learned that you don't end up with power just to say that you have it.

I have learned that it is possible to be obedient and still obstructed. That wasn't always my frame of mind. I used to think that if I was obedient, everything would be perfect. Now I realize that all things work for my good, because of my love for God and also because I am determined to hold onto His purpose. But, you can be in the will of God and still blocked.

This truth reminds me of the passage in Matthew 14:22-24.

Matthew 14:22-24
22 *Immediately Jesus made the disciples get into the boat and go on ahead of him to the other side, while he dismissed the crowd.* **23** *After he had dismissed them, he went up on a mountainside by himself to pray. Later that night, he was there alone,* **24** *and the boat was already a considerable distance from land, buffeted by the waves because the wind was against it.*

If you are familiar with the passage, this is the story where Peter walks on the water. It is arguably one of the most faith inspiring stories in the Bible. But there is another aspect of the story that we don't focus on as much.

Jesus commanded them to go to the other side, and they complied. They did not question Jesus, or rethink Jesus. They did not hesitate, as we often do, they immediately obeyed. This trip across the lake was not supposed to take long. But they were a considerable distance from land because the wind was against them.

I hope I just blessed you. I hope I just gave many of you an answer that the enemy has been plaguing you with. "If you are in the will of God, why aren't you there yet?" The next time you hear that from the enemy, you just remember that it is absolutely possible to be obedient and be blocked.

That is what a mountain is; a mountain is an obstacle, something in your path on your way to your destiny. That is why I am saying that Mark 11:23-24 is for movers. Jesus is talking to people who are on their way to another level. Jesus is speaking to people who have the courage to believe for more!

No one speaks to mountains just to be able to brag about how they spoke to a mountain. The power to speak to a mountain comes out of the faith and the determination to move on from where you are. And until you are actually there, until you are on your way higher and a mountain is looming, you may not really have that power.

Let's make sure we start off with a clear understanding. I am not trying to repeat myself, but I want to be sure that we are in agreement. You don't walk around with mountain moving faith and power in your pocket, just to have it. Jesus had the Spirit without measure. You and I, we have the Spirit with a measure. A part of what causes us to even speak to the mountain is the travel from glory to glory. You know where you are and you know where you want to be. The mountain is in the way. You must tap into the desire to move forward to muster the faith to move the mountain. And until you are facing that mountain, I am not sure if you have that power.

So the beginning is to get you to move. The start is for you to believe. Faith is the substance of things hoped for. What are you hoping for? What are you dreaming for? What is the desire of your heart? What has the Lord laid on your heart to do? Where are you going? What is your MORE?

We are Abraham's seed. Those of us with faith are of the seed of Abraham. I know we like to look at Isaac and receiving the promise, but the first thing that Abraham did was move. He moved from where he was to where God wanted him to be.

Later, after 400 years of slavery, Abraham's offspring found themselves on a journey, from Egypt, through the wilderness into Canaan.

Here we are, we are Abraham's heir. You have faith; you are of the seed of Abraham. You can't claim his blessing without claiming his mission and his actions. Faith is a journey. Faith is a path you take, it is a highway. Faith is the road you take to get to the impossible.

While you are on this journey, you are going to face some mountains. You are going to face mountains that everyone who takes this faith journey has to face. Anyone who walked by faith had mountains to overcome. I finally learned to stop fighting the mountains. I decided to accept them as part of the landscape of the mover! My assignment is to help you on that journey. That is what this book is about. I am going to help you to identify each mountain that stands between you and greatness. You are not by yourself. You are not the first person to take this journey and you will not be the last.

Please understand, hear me!

The journey to your destiny is not one that you will be able to get to without challenges. I have stopped complaining about mountains. I have to come to realize that mountains are going to be a part of my life's landscape. The road to your destiny is not a straight shot, it is going to be about overcoming the mountains in our way. And, it is also going to be about understanding why the mountain is there.

I know the minute you see a mountain in the distance, you immediately want to pull out Mark 11 and get to rebuking it. Believe me, I know where you are coming from. Although I am excited about the prospect of sharing my experiences with faith, I have to admit that it is easier to have that attitude when the mountain is at your back.

Even though we read the Word, go to church and learn to worship to develop this close relationship with God, I'm not sure we are truly interested in using this power for what it was intended for. I think we want nice level peaceful ground. If you are anything like me, when you see the mountain on the horizon, it may even seem beautiful, but you aren't looking to live there.

Why? Because mountains are nice to look at from a distance, but serious mountains, up close and personal; they can be extremely intimidating. Let's be honest, mountains are dangerous. Mountains are normally surrounded by forests and climbing them can be physically taxing and dangerous. There can be climate change on a mountain and the air becomes thinner as you ascend. In other words, climbing a mountain can kill you.

I have grown tremendously as a result of my struggle with mountains. But if I'm honest, I must admit, most often that growth was not my idea. I actually was not interested in any tangle with mountains. But I soon learned that mountains are going to be a part of my journey in life and more importantly, my journey to more. You have to learn that before you start rebuking, you need to first identify the mountain. This mountain that you are facing, where did it come from? Did the Enemy do this, or is this life? Sometimes I think we overly blame the devil for challenges.

I heard my father tell a funny story about the devil.

A man was walking down the street, and as he passed a church he saw the devil sitting outside on the curb crying. The man asked, "What is wrong Satan?" And the devil answered him as he pointed toward the church, "Those people in that church, they blame me for EVERYTHING!"

That's a cute story, but I am not sure it is an adequate picture of the enemy. I think he wants us to blame him because then we will never focus on the other sources of our difficulty.

There are mountains that have been placed there by the enemy. But my point is this:

Mountains have to be identified before they are spoken to. Before you start yelling at your mountain in the name of Jesus, I would suggest you do some "Mountain Examination." Different mountains require different responses. One of the biggest mistakes you can make is to treat all of the mountains the same.

Let's focus for a moment on what I will call...

The Right Response to the Mountain

1. Identify the mountain.
There are 5 mountains that we are going to identify in this book. Each mountain must be faced on your way to **MORE** and to the power that God has for you. And believe me, as the Word promises, your eyes have not seen and your ears have not heard and your mind has not conceived what God is prepared to do in your life.

I need you to believe that. Your latter days will be greater. This is not the period, this is a comma in your story. You need to keep this in mind so that you will keep moving from mountain to mountain, from glory to glory. Understand that as you deal with each mountain, your faith continues to increase. You can't run from these mountains, you have to deal with them.

2. Appreciate the mountain.

I know that this can sound insane, especially if the mountain is something very difficult and especially if the mountain has been placed there by the enemy. You know, I am at a place now where I often stand in awe of the brilliance of the enemy. I am dealing with something right now, a clear attack from the enemy. And as angry as I am about it, I tell you, sometimes you just have to give Satan his props. He sure knows how to put the perfect storm together. That is what I tell myself as I strap on my armor to go to battle. The weapons won't prosper, but that enemy sure does know how to form them.

Mountains have a way of making you pause for a moment. You can want to get to better so quick, that you can get lost along the way. You can be in such a rush to find love that you choose the wrong person. You can be in such a rush about business that you have not quite done as much investigation as you need to. The blessing of the obstacle is that it slows you down.

I was counseling a Pastor who was extremely upset over a leader that left his church. I know what that is like. But then I asked him, "but aren't you on your way to greater? If you are on your way to greater, isn't it better to lose disloyal people here at the lower place?" Sometimes betrayal is a blessing in disguise.

My point is this, the mountain needs to be appreciated and even respected. If you are being blocked by a mountain that your weakness or mistakes helped to build; then you need to savor this mountain for a moment, so that you will never make this mistake again. You can't just rush right past the mountain. The mountain deserves some respect.

3. Respond Appropriately

There are 3 major responses to the mountains that we will face or maybe better stated, there are 3 Ways To Move the Mountain.

A) Physical Mountain Displacement

When I say physical mountain displacement I mean the mountain actually is moved. This can happen to 2 ways. The first way is what we all want. It is what we assume when we read Mark 11:23.

You speak to the mountain, and by the power of God, the mountain gets up and moves into the sea.

And believe me, this is absolutely possible. We can speak to tumors and they have to move. We can rebuke cancer, disease, people and situations. I do believe in the power of prayer. I do believe that what you bind on earth God will bind in heaven.

But there is a second way that physical mountain displacement happens. The second way is God moves YOU.

When I was living in Boston, my hometown, there were some mountains that I started to bind and rebuke while I was there. There were some obstacles that were in my way. I knew that God had a work for me to do. I knew I was on a journey, but I was being blocked. I started speaking to those mountains, and I found myself in North Carolina. Those mountains are still there, but they are no longer a part of my life because God moved me.

Can He move you? Sometimes we want the Lord to change everything but us.

"Lord, touch my husband!"

"Lord, touch my supervisor. I bind him in the name of Jesus!"

"Lord do something about my neighbor, about my wife, about my cousin, about my mother-in-law!"

"God, fix them and leave me the same!"

I don't know what Abraham was praying about. I don't know what he was asking God for. But before he received any miracle, God moved him. Sometimes that mountain ends up behind you because you walked around it. Sometimes the mountain was there to show you that you were headed in the wrong direction. The mountain ended up at your back because you turned around.

Both methods have been a part of my journey. I have spoken to mountains and they have moved. And I have spoken to mountains; and God made me let go of some people, he caused me to refocus. He left the landscape the same and changed me.

B) Mountain Climbing

I have learned that some mountains are permanent. The Lord wants you to move the mountain by putting it under your feet. Perhaps, instead of rebuking the mountain you should grab a rope and start to climb it. Mountains aren't always a bad thing. Fortresses are built on the top of mountains. When you have a mountain fortress, you have a place that is easily defendable.

I have climbed many mountains and I have found that I can see things that I never would have been able to see if I had never climbed the mountain. The mountain that I wanted to curse became the very thing that gave me revelation. And the strength that I have gained as a result of the struggle was worth the challenge of the mountain itself.

At the top of the mountain, the air is thinner. But, when you train at higher altitudes it gives you a level of endurance that you would never have had without the mountain. Things that used to bother you and problems that used to affect you, are less potent when you come down from the mountain. You find that you have actually been strengthened by the mountain. And now, there are some mountains that I would never think about rebuking. When I first saw them I was bothered. But now, that has become my mountain. That struggle is the moment that defined me.

Some of your mountains are here to stay. Some of these mountains that we will outline, even if you could rebuke them, it wouldn't be smart. You need that mountain. You needed that mountain to help you to see where you were really supposed to be. When they first fired you, you believed that it was an obstacle to your financial health. Now you realize that God had something better for you. You were on your way to more! You wouldn't have been experienced the blessing if the challenge had not pushed you there. And now, you know that fear can never have you. That mountain showed you who you are and what you were made of!

C) Tunneling Under the Mountain
Some mountains have diamonds in them and some have gold in them. I remember a cartoon character that used to yell, "There's gold in d'em d'ere hills!" Who was that? Yosemite Sam? Well, imagine me in shorts with a long red mustache. I am yelling that at you. "There's gold in d'em d'ere hills. Before you rebuke the mountain, you may want to dig deeper, there may be riches in the mountain."

The mountains that I eventually tunneled under were so big that they slowed me down. I couldn't go around them, I couldn't rebuke them and they were too high to climb. So, the mountain made me go deeper and as a result, I found treasure inside the mountain. Some mountains cause you to dig your own well within yourself. There are certain mountains that make you get down to the bottom of you. The only way for you to get past it is to go deeper.

Sometimes we just want to gloss over challenges based on someone else's faith. We want to hear their story so that we can find their formula for success. Can I tell you a secret? That never works. Even if I tell you my formula, you will have to apply it to your life. And we are different. The formula is like a sword that has been made for you. It has a balance that fits your hand and your weight. You can't fight with Saul's weapons, you have to fight Goliath with what you have.

Thankfully, God is with you. He will never leave you nor forsake you. He will be your guide, even as you dig deeper into the depths of your own soul. You will find that there is treasure within.

As I said earlier, there are 5 mountains that we will identify in this book. Each mountain must be faced for you to get to MORE. The mountains are in a specific succession. It would not be wise to read the table of contents and then skip ahead to a mountain that you believe fits you. They ALL fit you. All the mountains have to be examined and if you are not successful in rebuking, overcoming, tunneling thru, climbing over or going around them, then you may never reach the ultimate will of God for your life. Ultimately, that is what I want for you. I want you to reach your destiny.

I have given you these 3 mountain movement tools because different mountains will require different approaches. For some, the Lord will have you go around that mountain, others, the Lord will have you climb that mountain. For some of you, the Lord is going to have you tunnel through that mountain and for some, God Almighty is going to intervene and remove that mountain altogether. No matter the how, you will overcome that mountain. Together we will get the mountain moved.

Just keep in mind while reading each chapter, that the first step is always identifying what that mountain is. We will begin in each chapter giving you a basic understanding of that mountain. Once we identify what the mountain is, we will determine if that mountain was put there by the devil, if the mountain is something that we've orchestrated ourselves or if the mountain in our way, has been put there by God. There are some mountains where it may be a combination of both. The Enemy attacked but God allowed it, to build you up. Or you made the mountain and the enemy has held it there. I won't be able to give you all of those answers, you will have to hear from the Spirit, but don't worry, He will speak to you.

Once the mountain is identified, you will have the courage to approach that mountain and accept it. The knowledge alone will help you. Mountain clarity from mountain confusion is often half the battle. Once you approach that mountain with full awareness of what the mountain is, and when the Spirit confirms for you how it got there, you will find the path to move that mountain. When you approach that mountain with the tools I'll give you and with the increased faith that comes from every victory over each mountain, you will begin to realize just how powerful you are in Christ. This process will endow you with the strength that only the Holy Spirit provides.

Please understand, that as you complete each chapter, you will be taking steps closer toward your destiny. With the conquering of each mountain, you are building momentum and getting closer to the greater God has in store for you.

Allow me to throw just a few more tools at you to help you with this journey. I would suggest that you be faithful in church, make sure you are tithing and make sure you are giving. If I were you, I would read this book with a journal to write in. You will need to take some notes so that this will be a moment of growth for you.

And remember some basics, what I call: **Faith 101**
Faith 101 is what Mark 11:22-25 recommends to all of us. These are the tools you will need for this book to really help you and ultimately the tools you will need for abundant life.

22 "Have faith in God," Jesus answered. **23** *"Truly[f] I tell you, if anyone says to this mountain, 'Go, throw yourself into the sea,' and does not doubt in their heart but believes that what they say will happen, it will be done for them.* **24** *Therefore I tell you, whatever you ask for in prayer, believe that you have received it, and it will be yours.* **25** *And when you stand praying, if you hold anything against anyone, forgive them, so that your Father in heaven may forgive you your sins."*

The TOOLS

A) Have Faith in GOD
This is going to be about the Lord. This is going to be about His power. We want to build you up in faith, but you are going to have to start with something. To have faith in Him you have to…
- Know Him
- Praise HIM – (Learn to Sense HIM)
- FOLLOW HIM

B) Use your Words
I remember saying this to my sons. "Use your words, stop grunting at me. If you want juice don't point at the sippy cup. Say, 'Juice please.'"

You will have to get your mouth on your side. To do that you will have to:
- Know the Word – pull up scriptures that you have memorized and begin to speak them to yourself

- Know YOUR word – Be specific about what you are believing God for. Go ahead, get it in your head right now. Whenever the going gets tough, focus on that thing. Which leads us to the 3rd tool:

C) Desire

Mark 11:24 in the King James version says, *"What things soever ye desire, when ye pray, believe that ye receive them, and ye shall have them."*

I love the word "DESIRE." Faith is not apathy. You Will Have to WANT THAT THING! You have to want MORE, want it more than you can be bothered by the pain to achieve it.

You have to imagine it in your mind. See yourself there – at the place God wants you. See yourself standing in destiny, standing in health, standing in wealth. You will never get there if it doesn't even matter to you. Pretending to not care is a defense mechanism that we use to try to protect ourselves from the pain of not attaining.

That won't work! You have to want it; you have to desire it. There has to be a longing, there has to be a desire. Desire gives your prayer a greater level of fuel.

D) Pray

Prayer has power. When you get your desire involved, your heart starts to pray. This is how you pray without ceasing. Even when your lips aren't moving, your heart keeps praying. But prayer is the key, your faith unlocks the door.

E) Believe Before You See

Are you ready to believe you have it even before you see it? It shouldn't be too hard because if you could see it you wouldn't need to read this book on faith. Believe that it is possible. Your next level is possible. Find your faith and know that anything is possible when you believe. Let's head down the path and face the mountains. You have no time to lose, but you have everything to gain!

Chapter 2

MOUNTAIN #1
The Personal Identity Mountain

Acts 19:13-16
13 Some Jews who went around driving out evil spirits tried to invoke the name of the Lord Jesus over those who were demon-possessed. They would say, "In the name of the Jesus whom Paul preaches, I command you to come out." 14 Seven sons of Sceva, a Jewish chief priest, were doing this. 15 One day the evil spirit answered them, "Jesus I know, and Paul I know about, but who

are you?" **16** *Then the man who had the evil spirit jumped on them and overpowered them all. He gave them such a beating that they ran out of the house naked and bleeding.*

"Jesus I know, and Paul I know about, but WHO ARE YOU?"

I think this question is probably one of the most non-answered questions in our current society. There was a time when your personal identity was a serious topic of discussion at the dinner table. I can remember my father telling us what Thompsons do, what Thompsons don't do and who Thompsons are.

"Thompsons don't get bad grades!"

"Thompsons aren't lazy!"

"Thompsons don't let their temper rule them!"

"Thompsons act like they have some sense, BOY!"

I remember thinking, "then I must not be a Thompson because my grades are bad, I don't feel like getting off this couch, you are starting to make me mad, and I kind of want to slap you, which makes no sense since you would kill me, so I am 0 for 4."

The point is, our parents weren't waiting for us to discover ourselves. They were determined to help us figure out who we were as quickly as possible. And they were right, because there is too much at stake in this thing called life for you to walk around not knowing who you are.

Therefore, it is more than necessary that we begin this journey with the mountain of YOU. I believe that this mountain is a *God placed mountain*, although I am sure that people and even the enemy could have had a hand in the confusion you may have about yourself. But believe me, once you dig into the mountain that is you, you will find a treasure that will forever finance your faith in God.

When you are done with this chapter, you will be well on your way to greatness and destiny. You will be strengthened against fear, and you will be ready to move further towards the amazing that you have yet to see!

When I first heard someone preach from Acts 19, the seven sons of Sceva, the story scared me half to death. I was about 7 at the time and everyone in the church back then was always thinking about demons. I heard some of my father's preacher friends say, "When in doubt, cast it out!"

People believed there was a demon in everything. I actually heard one of my dad's friends say,

"A demon in the sound system tried to stop my sermon today!"

I heard a woman give a testimony, and she said,

"The demon of running out of gas tried to stop me from getting to work, but I just ignored that blinking light and confessed the Word all the way to the office!"

Of course, we know that it wasn't a spirit in the sound system, it was problems with the system. Feedback is not an attack of the enemy. And if your gas light is blinking, you need to pull off at the next exit and go to the gas station!

When I was a kid, I used to go to sleep with a bible on my chest because I was so scared of demons. When I matured, and reread this story, it just confirmed a truth that I now preach consistently.

The enemy is real and when you confront him, you better know Jesus for yourself. AND...YOU BETTER KNOW WHO YOU ARE!

Jesus I know, Paul I know about, but WHO ARE YOU?

As I have already stated, I don't think this question is asked enough! We study so much in school, we learn so much, but we haven't quite taken the time to learn who we are.

In biblical times, you had to know what family you were from and which tribe? Your identity began with your people and with their history. You could quote your generational line. That is one of the reasons it is given in the bible.

Today, most children are being raised without a relationship with their own father; sadly, they do not know the history of their family. The age of information and technology has given us access to people at a level never seen before. It is possible to read about Brad Pitt and Angelina. We know everything about Beyonce but don't know anything about ourselves. We know about Trump, we know about Kobe, we know what Tom Brady eats for breakfast, we know all about celebrities, but are unaware of our own gifting.

Our biggest obstacle is personal identity? This is a mountain you can't rebuke, this is a mountain that has to be dealt with.

You can't get so deep into the bible that you are able to hide what and who you are. I would contend that the Word is here to help you know who Jesus is, and for you to learn who you are in Him. The accounts of people in the bible are a glimpse into who you can become, if you put your trust in God.

But it starts with an examination of what God is working with right now. When you say, "I am giving my all to God," what exactly is God getting? Do you know? Or are you giving Him something that you have not even examined?

A good place to start is this question:
1. Who Did They Say You Were?

Most of us formed an opinion about ourselves through the lens of other people. One of the things that made Jesus so uniquely distinctive, is that He was absolutely sure of who He was even though people were unsure about who He was.

This is challenging, because people's opinion of you can have a great effect on your opinion of yourself.
Questions beget more questions.

Once we ask, "who did they say you were?" We have to then ask, "who were they?"

Whether we are talking about your parents, your family, your friends, even people on the bus. You have to ask yourself, who defined you to you?

Were they qualified to define you to you?

My dad loves to say, "I don't take swimming lessons from drowning people."

I was in the barbershop the other day, and I was listening to single men tell a newly married man how he ought to act with his new wife.

"You need to let her know who is running the house!"

Finally, I looked up at him and said, "I wouldn't listen to single men talking about how to be married. This is why they are single."

But this is what we do. We let poor people define wealth to us. We let unhappy people define joy to us. We let unhappily married people define wedded bliss to us. We let unattractive people define beauty to us.

Who told you who you were? Were they successful? Where are they now? Did they know what they were talking about?

You have to find the *"theys"* of your past. Are you who they told you that you were? Are you the you they made you be, or the you that you were supposed to be?

I have found that even the most well-intentioned people were wrong about me when it came to me. This can be especially true with parents and I had great parents. I am determined to be a great parent. But sometimes, as parents, we advise based on who we are and not on what is best for the kid. Right now, there are so many things I do not want my children to go through. I don't want them to go through any of the things that I had to go through.

But what if that is what they need?

At the same time, it is possible to want them to be exactly like me and to do it because I did it. I may want them to go to the same school that I went to, or to work like I worked; to save like I saved or to marry young like I married young.

And as well intentioned as I may be, at the end of the day, it may not be what is best for them. My point is that we have to start this personal identity examination with a look backwards before we storm ahead forward.

Who did they tell you that you were?

2. When Will You Get HONEST with YOURSELF?

I believe that self-honesty is a sign of maturity. At some point, you have to get honest with yourself and face who you are and deal with you.

Have you ever been around someone that is unfamiliar with the use of mirrors? Right now, as I am writing this, in teenage, young people world, it is hip to be a bit grungy. Although my sons are 18 right now, I am so glad that I have been able to get them to see the importance of their appearance.

I am sure you have seen someone and you've thought, "they must not have looked at themselves in the mirror" or, "they must not be able to smell because they need a bath!"

I am amazed by this world of "NON SELF EXAMINATION."
No one wants to proof read his or her own material anymore.
Everyone wants to be an expert, despite his or her lack of
qualifications. People who have barely been married for 5
minutes want to advise others on marriage. People who have
accomplished little want to tell other people how to do great
things.

At some point, you have to get honest with yourself and face
who you are. Eventually, you have to come to grips with who
you are and who you are not. Sure, you have things to work on
and you are still growing and evolving, but there are some things
that you will never do well. The sooner you get honest with
yourself the better.

There are some things you need to be able to tell me about
yourself. You need to spend some time with you and date you!
Before you go chasing another relationship, let's focus on you
first. Figure out who you are, then you will be able to know what
you bring to the table and what you need.

Before you go asking God to make you king of the world, ask
yourself the question, "am I qualified to be king of the world?"
We can't just want something because we want it. You have to
first figure out if you are even ready for it.

This is mountain talk. This is MORE talk! Do you know
yourself?

I believe there are several things you ought to be able to tell me about yourself. And until you have gotten honest, until you have matured enough to answer these questions, you will stay obstructed and this mountain of self-identity will not move.

You often don't find out who you are until challenges come. Challenges define you and refine you. There are 10 things you ought to know about yourself. If I say to you, "tell me about yourself," you ought to have a lot to say. If I interviewed you, these are the questions I would ask to find out who you were.

If I was dating someone new, these are some of the questions I would want to ask to learn who they are and what's more, to see if they knew who they were. Here is my list:

10 Things You Ought to Know about YOU

1. What Are Your Strengths?
You ought to know what you do well. If you can sing well, then you ought to know that and you should to be singing. I recently heard a story about a young woman who is an excellent singer but she doesn't sing because of a bad experience she had as a child. Her father made her sing once when she was feeling sick and that experience affected her willingness to sing in public.

I thought to myself, how sad is that? You have a strength and now you never use that strength because of something that happened as a child. That is so sad!

If you do something well, then you should know. If you love people, you should know that. If you are a detail person, you should know that. If you are creative, if you can draw, if you are great at organizing people – all of these are strengths you should know about.

What were you born to do? What comes easiest to you? There are so many of us that are in a job that we hate because it is not our natural fit. Someone told you what you should be and you followed that advice and now you are at a place where you realize your job does not quite fit your strengths.

I was in a mall area and the mall security guard came over towards me. I nodded politely, but then he proceeded to start a conversation with me, that lasted for over 10 minutes. He was a talker.

I remember thinking, "why is this guy a security guard? He should be in a job where he talks to people!" He was one of the most genuinely friendly people I had met in some time.

There is almost nothing worse than being in a job you are not positioned for. Have you ever had a bad teacher? A bad teacher in school can almost ruin your academic career. I was a good student until I got to the 4th grade. My 4th grade teacher acted like she didn't like children and she soured me on going to school. She had a reputation; everyone knew how she was. When I was leaving the 3rd grade, during the summer when I was waiting to find out who my 4th grade teacher was going to be, I was terrified that I would get Ms. Horter. Sure enough, my dread was confirmed. She was someone who was in a job that was not built for her strengths. She should have been a warden at a prison.

My point is, you need to know what comes easy. That does not mean that there will not be work. But working hard at something that comes easy brings a different level of fulfillment. There is nothing like finding your niche, the reason that you are here on this planet and then giving it all you have.

You should be able to tell me what you do well. And conversely, you ought to be able to tell me:

2. What Are Your Weaknesses?

No one does everything well. At some point, self-honesty will require humility. What is it that you do not do well? If you can sing, then you should sing, but if you cannot sing, why try to be a singer?

When you are confident in who you are, you do not hesitate to admit that there are things that you do not do as well. Great people surround themselves with a team that is based on their strengths and weaknesses. If you are unable to admit that you have weaknesses, then how will you ever be able to assemble a team?

What are you working on? What aspect of yourself are you fixing? I am a work in progress. There are still things I am getting better at, so please be patient as I continue to grow. You have growing to do; you have maturing to do. Can you admit that?

The silent consequence of low self-esteem is the inability to receive criticism. When you are confident in who you are, you will seek out someone to help you sees the flaws that you cannot see. When you really love yourself, you love the good and the bad. Maybe love is a strong word. I don't love the fact that I am not a detail person, but I have learned to accept that as a fact.

Since I was aware of that weakness, I surrounded myself with detail people. The details are never overlooked because I am able to admit that I need help.

3. What Do You Need?

When I was younger, we used to sing a song that said, "Jesus is all I need!" It is a nice sentiment, but not quite the truth. We all have needs and you have to find out what need is driving you. I attended a seminar on needs. The presenter taught us that one of the things that all humans have in common is that we all have needs. He explained that there are 6 primary needs that all humans have.

He went on to explain that every person is driven by a primary and a secondary need. Think of it like a mini-van full of needs.

One is driving you and a second one is in the front in the passenger seat. The other 4 are in the back making some noise. You have all 6, but your primary and secondary needs are in control. You can trace your happiness or lack thereof, back to whether or not those needs are met.

Let me give you all 6 and then you can examine yourself to see what needs are driving you. Perhaps the cause of your depression is unmet needs.

6 Primary Needs of Humans

1. Consistency
Humans need consistency. We need the air to be consistent and the temperature to be consistent; we need the ground to be consistent and we need love to be consistent. We need some things that we know we can depend on. That is why we established laws and governments, to assist us in our need for consistency.

When consistency is your primary need, you like for things to be predictable. You get annoyed when you don't have a certain amount of money in the bank. You like to know what is going to happen next. You don't like surprises. You are looking for something and for someone that you can trust. Change makes you a bit nervous, because you crave consistency.

Ironically and paradoxically, the next primary need we all have is:

2. *Inconsistency*

Variety is the spice of life. If things are too consistent, we become bored. This is why we go on vacation, take a trip, ride a roller coaster, go for a swim, hang glide. We need excitement to spice up life.

To some people, this is the need that drives them. They live to travel; they are thrill seekers. They aren't interested in everything being predictable all the time; they love to be surprised. The danger is what draws them.

3. *Significance*

We need to matter. We have a need to make an impact. You have a desire for fame, for your name to be great. We want our time on this planet to matter. We want to be remembered.

When significance drives you, you are determined to do something great. Nothing will stop you, you want to be remembered for what you accomplished.

4. *Love/Family*

Humans are communal species. We can't live without each other. We need one another to survive. We need someone to talk to, someone to connect with. Did you see the movie Castaway? Tom Hanks drew a face on a volleyball so that he could have someone to talk to, because a human left in isolation will go insane. Humans need humans.

Maybe this is your primary need. You put your family first. Family and love is above your career, that was an easy choice for you. Family is the need that drives you.

5. Growth

We need to change; we need to grow. We have to learn and gain more knowledge. We cannot stay the same; we are looking for the progress that is required for us to have peace.

People driven by this need are always taking a class; they are always learning something new. When you talk to them, they will tell you about how they are learning a new language, they cannot sit still. They are driven by growth.

6. Charity

Humans have a genuine need to help others. Making a donation and giving someone a helping hand satisfies a need that we all have.

People who are driven by charity dedicate their lives to the service of others. Have you ever wondered how someone can live on the mission field in a 3rd world country? It is more than just a calling, there is a need that they have that is being met.

We spent quite a bit of time talking about needs. Let's close with these last two thoughts.

A) No primary and secondary need is better than the others. They are all important. The point is to know yourself.

B) It is possible for your primary needs to change over time. What drove you when you were younger may not be what drives you now.

LET'S GET BACK TO THE 10 Things You need to know about yourself:

4. What Do You Like?

When you define winning and success, what does that look like? What do you actually want out of life? It is one thing to understand your needs and another to understand your desires. In your perfect world, what are you doing? What does it mean to win?

I was taught to pray specifically. That whatsoever I desired when I prayed, that I should believe it before I see it. But I have to know what I desire. The Word promises to give me the "desires of my heart." You should be able to explain to someone the things that would make you happy. Specifically, think for a moment, what is it that you like?

5. How Are You Viewed?

In Matthew 16:13, Jesus asks His disciples, *"Who do men say that I am?"* If Jesus was aware of the misperceptions about Himself, then so should we. So, that is an excellent question, who do people say you are?

One of the most valuable lessons one can learn on the path to maturity is this...It is absolutely possible for people to view you differently than the way you view yourself.

Sometimes people misunderstand because of who THEY are. People can project their thoughts and attitudes onto you. They believe that what is true of them is true of you.

Sometimes people misunderstand because of a way that you carry yourself. I remember when people used to think that I was arrogant. Hearing that was troubling, but it was good to know. That "arrogant" perception was a mountain I had to conquer. And the beginning of it was hearing it. I had to realize there were some things that I was doing that made people believe that about me. Once I changed some of those things, that misperception changed.

Sometimes people don't misunderstand you, sometimes they are right. We can get frustrated over misperception, we can get even more frustrated by dead-on perception. Knowing what people say, even if it is wrong, is still wise on the way to destiny.

6. How Did You Get Here?

The philosopher George Santayana said, "Those who cannot learn from history are doomed to repeat it." You ought to know your own history. What is your most significant testimony? Are you caught in a spin cycle?

I stand amazed at how many people are in the spin cycle. Solomon said that like a dog that returns to his vomit, so does a fool to his folly. Can you imagine reheating vomit, throwing a Tupperware bowl full of vomit into the microwave to heat up for leftovers? Beyond just the disgustingness of vomit itself, why would anyone eat something again that made them sick in the first place?

You need to make sure you are not in a spin cycle. We are creatures of habit and unfortunately, we have a tendency to repeat decisions just in the desire for predictability. You have to spend some time examining your past. What was your mother like? What was your dad like? Are you about to marry someone just like your mother? Was that relationship healthy?

It sounds crazy, because it is crazy. But people who grew up being abused end up in abusive relationships later in life. Sometimes the challenge is mounds of familiarity that we have piled up over time to feel comfortable. Even when what we are comfortable with is damaging, it can be hard to break free from the familiar. As you examine your journey, take a look at your people's journey as well. My path to faith didn't really start with me. My dad, who I will continue to reference, was the one who started our whole family on the faith journey. And some mountains are mountains I inherited from him.

To move forward past this mountain, you have to know where you came from.

7. What Is Happening Right Now?

I believe that God brings all of us on a journey from Egypt to Canaan. Understand, there is always a wilderness between Egypt and Canaan. One of the worst things that can happen to you is for you to have a Canaan expectation in your Wilderness experience. That is what derailed the children of Israel. They grumbled and complained in the wilderness.

You have to identify where you are right now so that you can know how to level your expectations.

There is a saying of mine that has carried me far. If you use this, please give me credit. The saying is…

"Anything is Tolerable when it is Temporary."

My wife and I had triplets; those boys are 18 right now. They are good boys, but they still bring challenges. Those challenges are nothing compared to what they were when they were 3. But even now, those troubles are temporary.

If you had asked me about my marriage and how happy I was when the boys were 2, I would have told you, "Things will get better!" Actually, that is when the "Anything is Tolerable..." quote first jumped in my head. I had to focus on when they were going to be 6. I had to acknowledge the wilderness. My wife and I didn't get to spend a whole lot of time together at that time, so, that was the wilderness.

As long as you keep the faith and keep moving, you will get to Canaan. But you need to identify where you are right now.

8. Where Are You Going?

Where do you see yourself in 5 years? In 10 years, where are you? What is your plan? What is your final destination?

I know you are going to heaven, but where are you stopping along the way.

Thankfully we all have GPS on our phones now. But I am old enough to remember my parents planning a trip using a map. Have you ever started to drive even though you don't know where you are going? You cannot make progress without a destination.

Jesus' promise of mountain moving power was to people with a destination. You don't just rebuke mountains for fun. You rebuke them because they are in your way. But first, you have to choose a way and the destination determines the way.

9. Who Are Your Friends?

Who are your real friends? Not the people who admire you and not the people using you. Who are the people that will be there for you through adversity? When I was younger I wanted a lot of friends. But as I matured, I began to see the value of a few very good friends.

There is a story in Luke 5, where the disciples catch such a great number of fish, that they have to signal in their partners and both boats were filled to overflowing. When the Lord pours out that blessing that you don't have room for, who will you share that with? Who do you trust to share your pain with, knowing they will never judge you?

10. Who Are Your Enemies?

It's time to realize how amazingly attractive our enemies can be. Before your blessing comes through, you need to know who is with you and who is against you. So many people sleep with their enemy. I know because it has happened to me. I actually had to be betrayed by some people, just so I wouldn't take them with me to the next place of blessing God had for me.

I didn't leave them, they showed their true colors and left me. All along the way, I thought they loved me. Only to find that they loved only themselves.

This may be a strange way to end this chapter, but I think it is an important question to answer. And, it really is an excellent connection since our next chapter is actually about People.

There are 3 types of enemies that you have to let go before you go to this next level:

A) People Who Just Don't Know

They don't know how great you are. They don't know how great you are about to become. Their ignorance causes them to be an enemy to your destiny. You have to let them go!

B) People Who Mean Well, but the Results are Always Pain

These can be the toughest enemies to break free from, since they really are more an enemy to your destiny than they are an enemy to you personally. They might actually love you, but to be a winner, you have to cut free from the losers holding you down.

C) People Who Just Plain don't like You, for Whatever Reason

This last one may sound obvious, but there are people who are enamored with their critics. Some people are so determined to win over their detractors that they don't spend enough time with the people who actually love them.

There are some people that you will never win over. For whatever reason, everyone is not going to like you. Thankfully, you know you and you like you. You know who your friends are. You have learned from your enemies what you needed to learn.

Your enemies can show you where you are weak. Now that you have learned that, move on. Life is too short to chase your haters.

Did you get that? Did you answer those 10 questions? I know it was a lot, but it was good. Congratulations, you have made it past the first mountain. But this was a good place to begin! You have to know who you are!

Jesus I know, Paul I know about, but WHO ARE YOU?!! Now that you have identified this personal Identity Mountain, you are on your way to MORE. You are fearfully and wonderfully made, you are not an accident. Your parents decided to have you, but God decided to send you and He sent you here on a Mission! Know yourself! Know what you are capable of; know that you can do the impossible! With God all things are possible. The mountains are not as daunting when they are identified. When you discover who you are in Christ, you are ready to tackle anything that life can bring.

Remember what Jesus said in John 16:33
"In this World, you will have Trouble…"

In this world there will be trouble, meaning, there will be mountains.

"But take heart, I have overcome the world."

Jesus isn't even worried about the problems or the troubles. He has already overcome the world. And with Him living on the inside of you, what can stop you. By yourself, you would be in trouble, but take heart, you have Him on the inside. And with Him, you are a different you!

Chapter 3

MOUNTAIN #2
The People Mountain

Mathew 16:21-23

*21 From that time on Jesus began to explain to his disciples that
he must go to Jerusalem and suffer many things at the hands of
the elders, the chief priests and the teachers of the law, and that
he must be killed and on the third day be raised to life.*

*22 Peter took him aside and began to rebuke him. "Never,
Lord!" he said. "This shall never happen to you!" 23 Jesus*

turned and said to Peter, "Get behind me, Satan! You are a stumbling block to me; you do not have in mind the concerns of God, but merely human concerns."

Now that you have crossed that Personal Identity Mountain, you are ready for the next task. People. And that is why this is a journey and why you are moving in succession. To handle this mountain range called *People*, you have to know who you are. Thankfully, now you do.

Most of the time when you say, get out of the way," you are speaking to a person. The mountains we face on our way are an obstruction on our way to our destiny of MORE. Let me say again, it is possible to be obedient and still be obstructed. Mark 11:23 is a passage for movers. It is a passage for people who know where they are and where they need to be. You have to know that what God has for you is better. You have to believe that this is not the end of your journey. You have to be determined not to die in this wilderness, but to maintain the faith that you had in the beginning and keep moving.

He did not bring us out this far to take us back again. He brought us out of Egypt to take us into the promise land. And even if there are giants in the land, we will not allow those giants to thwart the plan of God for our lives. You have to keep moving. God has a plan for your life and you have to refuse to let anything stop you from that plan. Especially not…

PEOPLE!

One of the things that was uniquely distinctive about Jesus was that He walked above the actions and attitudes of people. Jesus was sure of who He was even when people were not sure of who He was. Jesus knew why He was here. He was on this earth for a mission and He refused to be obstructed.

We have to be determined to be like Him. The Word promises us that we will all change, that what we shall be has not yet been made known. Did you know that? What you shall be has yet to be made known. But when He appears, we get to be like Him, for we shall see Him as He is. I know that passage in 1 John 3 is about the 2nd coming of Christ, but let's apply it right now as well.

What you shall be is yet to be known. But the clearer you see Him, the more you will be like Him. One of the characteristics of Jesus is that He was not blocked by people.

When we look at this passage in Matthew 16, you can almost feel bad for Peter. A few moments before this he was proclaimed as the ROCK! He had just been commended for having a true revelation from the Father. Jesus had asked His disciples who they said He was, another indication that Jesus was above the actions and attitudes of people. Jesus was so above the opinions of people, that He asked His disciples to tell Him about the misconceptions about Him. But I digress...

The same Peter that stands and speaks clearly, "You are the Christ, the Messiah, the Son of the Living God," that same Peter is now being rebuked for being a stumbling block. Peter goes from encourager to obstacle in one conversation.

Isn't that just like people? The same people that love and honor you one moment can be the very people that seem to be obstructing you the next. Of course, we know that our wrestle is not against flesh and blood. But the thing about the enemy is that just as God touches people through people, the enemy does the same thing. If Satan wants to block you, he sends a person.

I am sure that one of the reasons Jesus answers so strongly is that Peter has tapped into Jesus' aversion to the cross. We know from Jesus' garden prayer that the cross and separation from the Father was not exactly on Jesus' favorite thing to do list. When Peter takes Jesus aside to tell Him that this will never happen, Jesus has to remove the obstacle.

I am sure you get my point.

When we go to identify what is holding us back, very often, that mountain is people. This can be particularly challenging since we need people. You need people, and people need you. You love people and people love you. If you spend too much time by yourself, you will go crazy.

Have you ever been around one of those spooky deep Christians who have clearly been by themselves too long? I know that we used to sing, "as long as I got King Jesus, I don't need nobody else!" And that is a nice idea, but after you leave church, you need some fellowship with the saints. The Word tells us in 1 John 1:9, "As we walk in the light as He is in the light we have fellowship with one another, and the blood of Jesus Christ His son cleanses us from all sin."

There is a cleansing that happens through fellowship. At the same time, you have to make sure that you are fellowshipping with the right people. Because, just as time with the right people can take you higher, time with the wrong people can pull you down. You have to look closely at your company because we have a tendency to attract what we are.

"Birds of a feather flock together" as it says in the book of Hezekiah.

Actually there is no book of Hezekiah and that phrase does not appear in the Bible, but it is still true. If you love being around dumb people, you need to check to see if maybe you may not be as smart as you think you are. If you love being around people who party, you probably love to party. If you love being with people who love the darkness, you probably love the darkness. If all of your friends are unsaved, then you need to check your spiritual birth certificate and make sure that God is your Father and not Lucifer.

65

As Maury Povich would say on the DNA test shows, "when it comes to the identity of Joe here who loves to fight and loves to cuss and never goes to church and has 5 children from 5 different women… Lucifer, you ARE THE FATHER!"

What common is there between light and darkness? 2 Corinthians 6, "what does a believer have in common with an unbeliever?" I don't know if you are going to walk on God's highway if you spend all of your time with people on the low roads. I know we live in a time where we don't want to judge people. "Live and let live" is the mantra of the day. But you need to judge yourself. You need to examine this mountain that is blocking you. Ask yourself, "is it people?"

Let's take a few moments to identify the kinds of people that can actually block you from your destiny in God. I don't want you to actually call them "Satan" like Jesus did with Peter. But you do need to be aware if someone is being used by the enemy to hold you back from a place where God wants you to be. We are not trying to attack people and I am not trying to get you to be against people. It is not that you are going to turn your back on everyone you know. But you do need to identify your mountain. And if people are holding you back, you at least need to be aware.

So, let's identify the different kinds of people that can be mountains that have to be identified. I like to think of these mountains as…People Mountains.

1. Bad Parents

I almost hate starting this by going after your mother. But your parents are a huge factor in who you are today. We didn't really spend a lot of time talking about them in chapter 1, but your parents have a large impact on who you have become. I trust that they were more of a help to you then a hindrance. But what are they today? Unfortunately, so many people have bad parents.

That does not mean that you cannot rise above them. My wife's mother was an alcoholic; she was barely there. That could have been her excuse to not reach greatness, but it ended up being the fuel that she used to overcome. I know that we can be defensive about our parents, but we need to be able to face the facts.

For some of you this is easy. You know that you had bad parents, especially if they abandoned you. My wife read this before you did, and although she is not happy about the fact that her mother was not there, it is the truth. But some of us can be so defensive that we are blind to the truth of what kind of parents we actually had.

In case you are wondering, let me just quickly give you a brief measurement for your parents.

A) Abusive Parents

Parents that were physically abusive, clearly that is mountain that you had to overcome. And their presence in your life today should largely be dependent on their level of repentance. When I say "physically abusive" I mean more than just spanking. Many of us born before 1980 were spanked as punishment. My parents definitely spanked us. But a belt on your backside is not the same as a punch in the mouth.

My father used to ask me how many whacks with the belt did I think I should get. Looking back on that now, I want to call that abusive, although I know it was not. But it sure was hatred. I mean what are you supposed to say? I usually just said my age. I said a really low number once, something like 3 and he said, "How about 3 x 3?" which ended up being 9 so I never said 3 again for sure.

My great grandmother in Virginia made me pick my own switch from the switch tree once. I wonder if that was what it actually was, a switch tree. I don't know what that bush was actually for, but grandma called it a switch tree. I used to pee on it to try to kill it, but that only made it stronger. But I digress…

Corporal punishment is not what I am talking about when it comes to physical abuse. Although there are some people that were abused in this way, so there can be a fine line.

Emotionally abusive is also a form of abuse. Thankfully my parents were the kind of people where, once they punished you for something, it was over. They didn't continually bring it up and brow beat you over and over with your mistakes. If that was how your parents were, then that was emotionally abusive.

Sexual abuse, or even being so unaware that they allowed it to happen, that is another form of abuse that so many people have to overcome. There are just so many ways that we can define parenting...

The real issue with your parents is how they are today. Sometimes parents have a hard time moving from Authority to Influence. There are 2 types of power, Authority and Influence, and when you are a child, your parent's power over you is Authority. They have all of the responsibility so they have all of the authority. But as you age and mature, that power becomes more Influential. And some parents can struggle with that.

Are you 35 and your mother is still trying to run your life? At some point your parents have to know their place. Parents can define you by them. They can try to make you live their dreams. It is something that has to be examined.

B) Parents that couldn't be Followed
Some parents just weren't a good example. Parents are the first "gods" that we worship. We want to be like them. We look like them and we start to act like them. What they think is important, we start to think is important. Unfortunately, we can start to pick up their bad habits and behaviors. Some of you are blocked by an example that you have always followed. Many times when we ask for prayer, we are asking God to break us out of a cycle that we didn't even start.

2. Bad Leaders

Unfortunately, there are a lot of people who get the title leader and they really are not qualified to lead. So many times I hear someone that is turned off from church, not because of God, or because of a disappointment, but because of a bad leader.

Bad leaders...

- Use authority to manipulate people
- Don't practice what they preach
- Are threatened by anyone else with strengths and gifts
- Have to be constantly praised
- Are overly critical of others while full of grace for their own actions.
- Lead when they don't know where they are going

Whatever you do, don't let a bad leader hold you back from worshipping God. The old mothers in the church used to admonish us to, "keep your eyes off of people and on Jesus." It is sound advice. A leader is great, but you have to follow them as they follow Christ. If they start to veer away from the will of God, then you have to keep following Jesus.

3. Church People

Most of Jesus' people problems were with the most religious people of the day. The Pharisees and the Sadducees and the teachers of the law, very often they were His biggest critics. Instead of recognizing that He was the Messiah, they doubted and eventually plotted and carried out His death.

When I read the bible, I cannot quite understand what kept them from seeing who Jesus was. But the greater lesson I've learned from this is, you can't be surprised when you have a gift and people miss it. You cannot be swayed by the doubts of people. You have to know who you are. Faithfulness and stubbornness can be the flip sides of the same coin. What it takes to be faithful has a bit of the stubborn mixture in there. As a church planter, who was raised in a denomination, I see both sides of the issue. People in a denominational church have a tendency to be very faithful and loyal to that church. This is the church they grew up in, it is the church their parents attended. They will stay committed to that church, even if they do not agree with the Pastor. And they want the church to meet their needs. They may not be interested in changing to get new people, thus it can be difficult to get the church to grow.

But they are faithful.

On the other hand, you have the new churches, the start-up churches. As a church pioneer, I love the flexibility and how quickly a new concept can be implemented. At the same time, people are not as faithful as they were in the older traditional church. It used to be hard to lose people, but now, people leave for the smallest reason.

My point is, faithful consistent people can be threatened by change, and that is what Jesus brought. But even the disciples that shouted, "Hosanna!" fled from Jesus when He was arrested.

71

The same people that praise the loudest can also become passionately opposed to you at another time.

There are many people who have just enough religion to never really get Jesus. It is almost like the flu vaccine. They give you just a bit of the flu, just enough so that you will be inoculated against the real thing. There are many religious people just like that. To accomplish great for God, you have to overcome the mountain of religious people.

4. Close People who Hurt You

Unfortunately, many of us have a Judas or 2 in our pasts – people who got close to you, people that you thought you could trust, and they were the ones that hurt you the most. The enemy used them to get close to you so that they could betray you.

They have to be identified and forgiven. We talk a lot about Judas Iscariot, without remembering that without Judas there is no cross, and without the cross there is no resurrection. The glory of resurrection comes at a price, and often that price is betrayal.

The difference is that Jesus knew all things so He knew who Judas was and what Judas was going to do. Most of us are caught off guard by the Judas in our company. Once you identify Judas you have to know what to do.

At this point I have been betrayed so many times that I am starting to develop calluses on my back. There is nothing worse than for your good to be called evil, but if it happened to Jesus then it can happen to you.

There is a reason Jesus told us to forgive, to pray for our enemies, to be sons of God. When you decide to move on from the people that hurt you, 3 things happen:

3 Results of Forgiveness

A) You are able to move forward in your journey. You cannot move on holding on to someone that hurt you in your past. You have to forgive them, especially people who aren't even thinking about you anymore. You cannot let them be a mountain that blocks you from your blessing.

B) You stay open to new people. I know that one of the reasons for the Judas is to try to close you off from your Paul. I have to forgive so that the Lord can bless me with the disciple that will not betray me. The enemy wants you closed off. He doesn't want you to ever trust anyone ever again. He wants you to spend the rest of your life alone. You have to forgive your ex so that you can be open to new love. You have to forgive the friend that stole from you, so that you can be open to the friend that will bless you. Whatever you do, stay open. Don't let past hurts shut you down.

C) You Show that You are a Child of God, walking with Jesus above People. I recently did a funeral for one of the charter members of my church. The church was full of people who used to attend our church, but have since moved on. One of my friends asked me, "how did you react when you saw people that left you?" I understood his question, but this is where so many of us miss the victory. The best way to be is above what people do. I greeted them, I hugged them. Why would I be upset? The church is doing better than ever. If God is for you then what can man do to you.

The fact that I was like that helped God to get glory. I got a chance to be like Jesus, to be above the actions and attitudes of people. It is what we all have to do. We have to be above Talkers and Enemies and Evil People. I could keep listing people that are mountains until I ran out of paper. The aim is to be above them. So I want to spend the last bit of this chapter addressing a how question.

That How Question is: How Can I Be Delivered from People?

This sounds horrible, so let me start with that disclaimer again.
- You Need People
- You have to be around People
- You Love People and People love you

I am not suggesting that you become a hermit and abandon society. What I am suggesting is that we all have to figure out how to be like Jesus. How to walk with people and live with people and eat with people and love people and even die for people, while all along remaining above the actions and attitudes of people.

We come to church and ask God to deliver us from everything, from drugs, and alcohol, from sexual addictions and carnality, from the love of money and perversion. And those are laudable desires. But I also want us to ask God to deliver us from people. So let's jump in and finish this chapter strong.

How can You Be Delivered from People?

1. BE BATTERY OPERATED

Jesus had His own battery. His energy to act and react with people was not dependent on the people. His power came from within.

One of the problems with us is that we have a tendency to get WAY TOO MUCH energy from OTHER PEOPLE. We are like a lamp that has to be plugged in, and people are the extension cord. Our light is supposed to shine, but we are dependent on people to give us the power to shine.

If people like us, and praise us, then we just light up like a Christmas tree. But if people are upset and angry with us and critical of us, we can get very dark and down and depressed. And when I say we, I mean me too. Even as I am writing this I am saying, "Lord help me!"

There is no way a person should be able to ruin your whole day. There is no way someone should be able to ruin your whole week. We all have a choice to make. You can walk in Victory or you can skulk around in "Victimy". "Victimy" is a word I made up, I'm hoping it becomes a word. It means that you stay a victim forever.

As much as I have compassion for people who have been through something, at the same time you can start your life story from the same dark place forever. You cannot let the abandonment define you. Maybe you were molested, maybe you were abused, maybe you were raped, but is that now going to be a mark that you carry for the rest of your life?

I recently went to see a movie, where at the end, the main character said to his nephew, "I'm never going to beat this!" The story was tragic, what he had been through was horrible, but I was annoyed by that sentiment. I don't care what has happened to you, at some point you have to decide to live again. You owe it to yourself and you owe it to the person that hurt you. You have to show them that they didn't take your spirit from you.

Can you imagine Jesus depressed because people were mad at Him? Can you imagine Jesus refusing to get out of bed?

John comes in and says, "What's wrong Jesus?"

And Jesus responds, "I'm just having a tough day. I was telling the people that if they hold to my teachings they would really be my disciples and then they would know the truth and really be free and they just went crazy. Some of them called me demon possessed, some people were picking up stones! Picking up stones to throw at me! Can you believe that?!"

Then John says, "Hey Jesus, maybe you just need a nap. Just lay back down, I am going to make you a bagel with some mint tea and you just need to watch Survivor Egypt. I recorded the first 3 episodes, it is great. They had to climb a pyramid, actually climb a pyramid. You can think about being the Messiah on Monday, just take the weekend off."

"Thanks John," Jesus replied, "these Jews man, why don't they like me?!!!"

I know I went a little far with this play, but you get my point. Like Jesus, we have to have our own battery. The aim is not to be a lamp but to be a flashlight – to be able to go anywhere and the source of your joy and strength not be the approval of people.

1b) The Spirit is Your BATTERY

I want you to think of yourself as a car. The Spirit is your battery and the Word and Prayer are your ALTERNATOR. The alternator keeps the battery charged. As long as you spend time in prayer and spend time studying the Word, your battery will never lose charge.

Church is the battery / alternator check-up. We will give you a jump if you need it, but you shouldn't need a jump start every Sunday. You have to take the power of God home with you. You have to know the Lord for yourself. You have to wake up in the morning and turn on your alternator, sing songs, hymns and spiritual songs to the Lord. Set aside a devotional time so that God and His Spirit becomes the engine to your interactions with people.

That doesn't mean you start to act spooky and spiritual with everyone. It simply means that your power comes from within, not from people.

2. KNOW WHO YOU ARE

As we said earlier in the chapter, Jesus knew who he was, even when other people were unsure about who He was. Is that much easier said than done? Most definitely, because people's opinion of you can have a very powerful effect on you. But you can actually become even more assured of who you are when the attacks come.

One of the most familiar passages in the bible is John 13, where Jesus washes His disciple's feet.

John 13:3-5: 3 Jesus knew that the Father had put all things under his power, and that he had come from God and was returning to God; 4 so he got up from the meal, took off his outer clothing, and wrapped a towel around his waist. **5** *After that, he poured water into a basin and began to wash his disciples' feet, drying them with the towel that was wrapped around him.*

When You Know Who You Are...

You Can Serve

I often say to the wives in my church, your femininity must not be very strong if making your man a sandwich totally destroys it. I can't believe you worked that hard for your marketing degree and then simply bringing him his plate destroys your education.

I say to the men, if washing dishes makes you weak, you weren't much of a man to begin with. If changing a diaper robs you of your masculinity, then you weren't that much of a man to begin with.

Jesus knew that the Father had put all things under His power. He knew what He could do. Jesus knew He was from God and was returning to God. Washing His disciple's feet was born out of that confidence. If you are going to stand against public opinion, then you will have to know who you are.

People can talk

I was talking to one of the Bishops that I am under. I was complaining to him about an accusation that was made against me by someone that was very close to me at the time. After I had gone on about it for about 15 minutes, he finally asked me, "son, is it true?" When I responded that it was not true, his next question was, "then why are we talking about it?"

Isn't it amazing how a lie can distract you from your goal? The lie can become a mountain. It is not that it is so big that you cannot get around it, it is that you are so focused on the lie, that you are distracted from your journey. But when you know who you are (we covered this in the first chapter) it helps you to rise above the actions and attitudes of people.

You have to know when you are right and know when you are wrong. You have to examine yourself. You have to keep working on yourself. When you are working on you, no one has to point out the speck or plank in your eye. And even if they do, you are not bothered because you are already aware of the work that you need to do on yourself.

You have to know what motivates you. When someone questions your character, it can be very painful. But then, when you remember who you really are, the misunderstanding rolls off of you like water off of a duck's back. You find out how confident you are in who you are. Your energy comes from within, from the power of you knowing and having confidence in the YOU Christ has made you to be.

3. UNDERSTAND PEOPLE

Jesus was able to forgive people because He understood people. He prayed from the cross, in Luke 23, "Father forgive them for they know not what they do." Jesus knew what was in the hearts and minds of people. He knew their thoughts.

Now we do not have that power. Thank God! I don't think anyone would be married if we could read each other's minds. No one would have a job and your mother would have killed you if she could have read your mind. My mother didn't even like the face I was making half the time.

"Fix Your Face BOY!"

God, imagine if she could have read my mind.

We can't know people's thoughts, but we can understand people. If you are sitting here thinking, "I can't understand people," then you need to do a bit more people study. I believe people need to be watched for a bit before they can be trusted. Believe me, I am not trying to sound like a paranoid nutcase but I have been on the planet long enough and I have read the bible enough to know that you have to be careful before you start giving everyone your trust.

My daughter watches reality shows where couples meet and give each other roses or whatever and "fall in love." Notice that I put "fall in love" in quotes because I do not believe 6 weeks or 8 weeks or even 12 weeks is enough time to know if you are in love with someone. And it certainly isn't long enough to know if you want to spend the rest of your life with someone.

Since you can't read people's minds, you have to judge them by their fruit. Jesus said you will know people by their fruit. We have such a tendency to judge people by their gifts, that we don't take the time to see what kind of fruit they produce. A lemon tree is pretty, but that cannot be the only fruit you will eat for the rest of your life. I know a lot of men who married a lemon tree. I know a lot of women who thought they had an oak and the man ended up being a weeping willow tree.

People need to be watched and then people need to be categorized. One of the biggest mistakes you can make is to expect the same thing from everyone. Very often the measure of our discontent can be found in the measure between what we have and what we expected.

I've learned to categorize people so that they won't surprise me. Let me make a few category suggestions for you to help you in this area.

Some People are:

A) Good

In spite of it all, there are some genuinely good people out there. And when I say good, I don't mean just knowing how to put on a good face, I mean good all the way to the core.

When you meet someone good, you have to make sure that your bad experiences with people that are not so good, don't cause you to treat good people like they are bad people. I know that sounds obvious but it happens all the time. Good people pay the back tax for all the mean people you have had to deal with.

B) Hearts Are in the Right Place

Some people mean well, but the result is more often pain than not. I have plenty of people like this in my life. I know they love me, but a lot of the time they see me for what I can give and not how they can be a blessing to me.

Fortunately, I am never bothered because I know what they are bringing to the table. They come with need.

C) Immature

Have you ever had an argument with a 3-year-old? My 3-year-old granddaughter asked me for what she termed "Floop Loops" which then turned into a discussion about what they were actually called. She almost had me convinced until I remembered I could read. Sometimes people think something just because they still have growing to do.

Do you remember when you were 16 and you thought you knew what you were talking about? You thought that, until you turned 21, and then you realized how foolish you were. Then you turned 30, and the 30-year-old you was angry at the 21-year-old you. Do I need to continue? This never ends because there is always more to learn, there is always another level of maturity to reach.

I have decided that I am no longer going to let my neck get hot over something someone immature has said. Father forgive them, they are only 22.

D) Crazy

Some people are crazy. I don't even have to listen, I can hear the "Amens" coming through the pages. Everyone has some crazy people around, everyone has some crazy people in their family. And if you cannot think of anyone in your family who is crazy, you might want to look in the mirror.

People can say things that don't make any sense at all. You will be talking until Jesus comes trying to get them to see sense. My counsel is just smile, pray and walk away. Wow, I have never said that before. That sounds great. Let's say it together. How do we handle the crazies? Smile, Pray and Walk away.

E) Evil

Unfortunately, there are some evil people in this world. Joseph said to his brothers in Genesis 50, "you intended to harm me, but God intended it for good." Aren't you glad that everything is working for your good? I try not to focus too much on evil people. I know they exist, but thankfully I am covered by the blood.

4. Respond to the Category

As I said earlier, you have to stop trying to be the same with everyone. We have to stop expecting the same from everyone.

People need to be treated according to the way they have shown you. They show you who they are and then you should act accordingly.

The key to it is, truly understanding Love.

You have to love everyone, but understand there are different levels of Love. Think about it, it just makes sense. The Word tells us to love our enemies. But you aren't going to love your enemy the same way you love your friend or your child.

So let's wrap up this chapter with a quick refresher on Biblical love.

A) AGAPE – GOD'S LOVE
The first kind of love is, Agape, God's love. In my estimation, Agape is the most general and broad type of love. It is unconditional love. When Jesus tells us to love our enemies, He is talking about Agape love. It is a love that is not dependent on what you do. I tap into the love of God, and I can show you His love, even though I don't know you. I can honestly say I love everyone. I love you and I don't even know who you are. Actually, you bought my book so I really do love you. Maybe there is another biblical love.

How about we call what we have "Booklical" love? I just made that up, but that is what we have, you and I. I wrote this book and you bought it. You love this book so much you buy several

85

more copies and give them to people. And I love you so much I name my next child "Everyone."

We have to be careful about Agape love. It is wonderful, but it is very general. It is the foundation for love, but there are more levels.

B) EROS – ROMANTIC LOVE

Romantic Love is the most unique. You only have it with one person. It is the most intimate of love and is the love that is the most conditional.

One of the worst things you can do in your romantic relationship is to treat that person with Agape love. Of course you start with unconditional love. But understand, unconditional love is distant. If I start to expect unconditional love from my wife, then I may begin to continually violate her conditions. If I don't meet her conditions, if she does not meet mine, even if we stay married, we can lose our romantic love.

This is why so many couples are unhappily married. You introduced Agape love and began to take the person for granted. Romantic love is wonderful and special but like a fire, it has to be maintained or it can go out.

C) PHILEO – FAMILY LOVE

The most permanent and lasting love if Phileo. When you start to love a friend like a brother or a sister, your relationship has gone to another level. When your Romantic love turns into Marriage Covenant, you are in essence moving into family love. That is why you should share a last name. You have now decided to be family.

And one of the most grievous wounds can come from putting the family label on someone before you really know them, and then they rip themselves out of your life and leave a hole there that has to heal.

There is some family that you are born into, and then there is your real family. The people that you have decided to allow into your walls, the people that you actually eat and interact with.

You will never treat an enemy like a brother. You may be determined to love them, and certainly, I do love my enemies. But I have enemies that I love, that I never want to see again. I forgive them, but that does not mean that they are supposed to be a part of my forever.

5. Be CALLED

Everything changes when you seek the Kingdom first. When you understand and acknowledge that there is a call on your life, you begin to have a different attitude towards people.

A part of the power of the kingdom is being used by God to reach others. What happened to that? What happened to the determination to be used? I remember when a significant aspect of being a Christian was a determination to be careful about your witness.

Today we are so much about freedom and so intent on our needs being met, so driven after blessing, that we have somehow strayed from why Jesus called His disciples. He said, "follow me and I will make you fishers of men."

When you accept the call of God to fish for men, your perspective about men changes. Knowing that Jesus loved people enough to die for them and then accepting the call to that message, requires that I have a patience that I may not normally have. I love you with Agape love, because that love draws you to Him. I love you because He first loved me. I love you because that is how I know that I have passed from death to life, that is how I show that I am truly a disciple, if I love my neighbor as I love myself.

At some point, I realize that Jesus shed His blood for people. And if people are good enough for Jesus, then they are good enough for me.

2 mountains down, 5 to go. Keep at it! You are doing a great job. You have to keep taking each mountain step by step to get to MORE. And we will keep tackling a mountain in every chapter. I know this People Mountain was a tough one.When you realize that people may be keeping you from your next level, you must cautiously take action. You must be determined not to hurt them,

while at the same time, keeping them from hurting you. Your example is Jesus. He walked above the actions and attitudes of people. Hold His hand and walk with Him, and you will find that people will not be able to stop you.

You are getting closer to greatness with every chapter, with every mountain. Let's keep going! On to the next mountain!

Chapter 4

MOUNTAIN #3
The Mountain of Purpose

Jeremiah 1:4-5
4 The Word of the Lord came to me, saying, 5 "Before I formed you in the womb I knew[a] you, before you were born I set you apart; I appointed you as a prophet to the nations."

Once you have dug into who you are, and added the right people and removed the wrong people, it is on to purpose. You are ready to establish your fortress on the mountain of purpose. This fortress could not be built until you knew who you were. This fortress could not be completed until you knew who to give keys to and who to lock out. Now, you are ready for perhaps my favorite mountain in the range. You have to be about your PURPOSE!

I believe that God had a conversation with you before He sent you here. Just as with Jeremiah, the Lord knew you before you were formed in the womb. That is why the Word compels us to be reconciled to God. When you are born again, you rebuild a connection that you had with the Father before you were sent here. And a part of the work of the Spirit is to remind us of what the Lord has said to us.

Think about that for a moment. You had a conversation with the Father, you just don't remember it. The process of being born and then raised in flesh can cause a disconnect with your original purpose. I believe that you are not an accident. Your parents decided to have you, but God decided to send you. He sent you here on a mission.

The real you, is a spirit being. God sent you here into this flesh and you are here for a purpose. Finding that purpose and rediscovering your reason for being on the planet, can be one of the biggest obstacles on your path to greatness.
Isn't it interesting, we have started by identifying mountains, and 2 of the first 3 have to do with you. I trust that you find that

liberating. It means that your life is not in the hands of other people. Even though we just finished a chapter on people, ultimately people are not in control. The only one who should be in control of your destiny is God and YOU.

When I was a kid, 8 years old, I used to love to go to the amusement park. I loved all of the rides, except for the ones that spin you. Too much spinning made me motion sick, but I loved all the other rides. There were 2 rides that were my favorite. My number 1 favorite ride was the bumper cars, although I hated when people bumped me. I just liked to find the fastest car and then ride around on the outside of the track and practice my driving. I would put my right arm around my invisible wife and drive with my left hand. I would get on that ride over and over again. My mother would just leave me there. And I was great as long as no one bumped me, like my brother Matthew who loved to aggravate people. MATTHEW!!!

The other ride that I loved was a rocket ship that went around but it had a control stick in the front so that you were in control of how high you flew. Although the man at the control box determined how long the ride went, I was in control of the height of my ship.

I trust you get the connection. God is in control of how long this ride lasts, but I want to be in control of how high I fly. You want to be the one with your hand on the control stick. You have submitted your life to Him and now He is here to lead you and guide you as you navigate through this journey called life.

You will be forever lost if you are not able to be connected to your purpose in being here. It is a mountain that must be tackled, the mountain of purpose. But as with so many of these mountains that we are identifying here in the beginning of this book, this mountain has to be conquered, it cannot be rebuked.

So how do you conquer this Purpose Mountain?

I know for me, the mountains that I face have a way of slowing me down and causing me to make sure that I am where He wants me to be. I wish that you could just run on a flat track, but if you are reading this book you have discovered that life is an obstacle course. Something has come your way, and the only way to get past it is to:

REMEMBER Why You Are Here!

Very often, what you are facing is directly connected to why you are here. So it doesn't make a lot of sense fussing and getting annoyed over today, when today is providing you with weapons for tomorrow.

I often wonder if David ever complained about the lion and the bear attacks. I wonder if Jesse ever said, "How's it going out there with those sheep?"

And David said, "I don't know Dad, every time I turn around some lion is after one of the sheep. I got all of them stable, led them to the water, everything looked great. I pull out my harp, start working on my album project, and boom, out comes a lion. It is so frustrating!"

Can't you hear that conversation? But the minute David heard Goliath's challenge he realized why he had spent the last 10 years fighting "lions and tigers and bears, oh my!" He realized that all along he had been walking in his purpose.

You have to REMEMBER WHY YOU ARE HERE!!! YOU ARE LOOKING FOR MORE!!!!

This light and momentary trouble is achieving for you an eternal glory that far outweighs the trouble. You are being prepared for something great. There is a work, a purpose that God has for you. And when you climb the mountain of purpose, everything else becomes clear.

So…What is your Purpose?

There have been some great books written on purpose. I don't want to reinvent the wheel and repeat all of the great information we have gotten on purpose in the last 10 years. But allow me to add my 2 cents in on the purpose discussion.

1. Specific purpose begins with General purpose.

Before you get to be a Navy Seal, before you get to be in the Green Berets, before you become a specialist, you start off in the general military with everyone else. Once you show that you can march like everyone else and salute like everyone, then you are recognized for the special gifts you bring to the battle.

This is a part of the challenge. We want to be individuals from the very beginning. We want our special gifts to set us apart without first showing that we can answer to the leader in a group. If you want to find your purpose, start by being faithful. Who do you answer to? Is there someone that can tell you anything? You can't have all of this specialized authority and you aren't under any authority yourself.

Every church that talks about Vision has to begin by acknowledging that we have a common vision that Jesus sets. We are about to have a Vision Sunday at WOCC in a few weeks. Only in embracing the whole can we find the uniqueness that we search for as individuals.

2. Original Purpose is found in the Original Design process.

In other words, if you want to know why something is there, ask the designer. Take a look at the actual design process. When we look at animals, we look at the specifics of their structure and that gives us a glimpse into what they were designed to do, how they are equipped to survive.

I love the nature shows on the Discovery channel. I have a tendency to cheer for whoever is the subject of the show. So, if the show is about lions, then I am cheering for the lions to catch the wilderbeasts. If the show is about the Nile crocodile, I cheer for them to catch the zebras as they cross the water. But if the show is about the zebra, then I cheer for the zebra.

Anyway, when you watch those shows, you can see the way animals have evolved to survive in the environment. You and I know that God created the animals and gave them abilities that aid them in their fight for survival. And the same is true with us. To know why we are here, to understand our collective purpose, we simply have to look back at the design moment. Your Original purpose is found in the original design process.

And that is one of the reasons that Evolution has become so prominent. The enemy is determined to rob you of purpose. If we are all just some big cosmic accident, then why are you here? If you can be kept from a mission of purpose, then your life can become devoid of meaning. And nothing makes the enemy happier than a life without meaning. Thankfully you and I know the truth. You were created by an intelligent designer. You are here on a mission. Have I said that enough? Is it in your spirit yet? You have a purpose; you have a mission. Until you know what that purpose is, the unknowing will be a mountain that will forever keep you blocked from great. You won't have to blame the devil; you will be able to point the finger at your own lack of direction and purpose.

The Word says this in Proverbs 29:18 (KJV)

"Where there is no vision, the people perish: but he that keepeth the law, happy is he."

I have actually seen this passage in several translations. They all maintain the same sentiment. You have to be careful not to live a life devoid of purpose. You need to know what your purpose is.

One translation, the Young's Literal Translation says, "Without a Vision is a people made naked..."

In other words, a lack of purpose will bring a level of exposure that you may not want. You are covered by purpose. Aren't you glad for clothes? Aren't you glad the person you see in the mirror right out of the shower is not the person that people see at work? Thank God for clothes and thank God for Purpose.

To find our collective purpose, let's take a look at the original design process. If we want to know why we are here, we just need to look at the creation story. When I look at how God created us and specifically what He said to Adam and Eve when He created them, I see,

7 Purposes of Creation

Actually, I think of the purposes as rights. If God created Adam and Eve for a specific reason then you have a right to it. You have to fight for your rights. You have a right to expect everything that God promised them. Everything that God said to them is connected to your purpose. Every command that God gave them in Creation is yours by right.

This is a moment to be empowered! This is a moment to fight the good fight of the faith. Fight to take hold of that for which Christ took hold of you. If Adam and Eve had it, then so should you. In this design account we find our purpose, and the key to identify the 3rd mountain.

We find the first 3 in Genesis 1:28

28 *God blessed them and said to them, "Be fruitful and increase in number; fill the earth and subdue it. Rule over the fish in the sea and the birds in the sky and over every living creature that moves on the ground."*

1. BE BLESSED

Genesis 1:28 says, "God BLESSED them…" When God created Adam and Eve, He created them for blessing. He didn't create them for curses, He didn't create them for challenges, He didn't create them for lack. When He decided to make man in His own image, it was a good thing. At the end of each creation day, God calls it a good day. Therefore, when He created mankind, that was a good day. The creation of man was meant to be a blessing to man. Why create us just for us to endure an existence of pain.

Although there is trouble and difficulty in this world, that was not the original purpose and intent of God for man. His intention was to bless us and in that we find our purpose.

1a) You are Here to be Blessed! Say that to yourself. "I am here to be blessed! Life is supposed to be a blessing!" Did you say it? Good, it is a good confession to make. No matter what has happened in life, you should always expect better. Hebrews 11 says that faith is the substance of things hoped for. You have to know what you are hoping for. You have to keep your eyes fixed on the better that life will bring.

There are some that want to purport an idea that life is tough, that life is suffering, that life is pain. Some people come to expect difficulty out of life. Have you ever heard the saying, "_____ Happens!?" I can't say the actual word. It is a swear word for crap. I am not even sure if I should say crap. But I said it, even though I am a man of God and this is a Christian book. I am sure you have heard the saying. Subsequently, I agree, crap does happen. But when it happens to me, I take that crap and use is for fertilizer. If right now it is raining crap in your life, then thank God. You are going to have a huge harvest. I know because I have had so much crap tossed at me in the last year, I know my seed is going to grow.

My point is, the challenge does not define life for me. In this world we will have trouble, but I will bless the Lord at all times because I know that it will work out for my good. God did not design me for a life of trouble. He created me to bless me, so blessing is a part of my purpose. I am always searching for my next level of blessing. The challenge you are facing is setting you up for your next level of blessing. I know that God has something better. Even if that better is heaven, praise God! Even death has no sting when I know that I am going to live with Him in a mansion in the clouds. My expectation is for greater; my expectation is for better. You have a right to expect more than what you have right now. The beginning is blessing!

1b) To BE a Blessing

A part of your purpose is to be blessed so that you can be a blessing to others. I was talking to God the other day, and I said to Him, "Lord, if I am generous right now, imagine how generous I will be when you set me free from debt!"

I am not trying to be blessed so I can sit around and count up all my blessings. I am not asking God for wealth so that I can see how much I have and be happy. You will find a new level of confidence in His plan to bless you when you are determined to help someone else.

A part of your purpose is to be a giver. You should be generous on every occasion. Give to the needy, support children in poverty, faithfully pay your tithes and give offerings. You will find that purpose start to come alive in you. Even if you are not as happy with your job, if your job provides you with the means to be a blessing, then your job may not be as tedious. Believe

me, when you help someone else, you get connected to the plan of God for your life. God touches people through people. If you just start to help people, if you just start to be a blessing to people, you connect with the purpose of God for your life.
Life is supposed to be full of laughter and joy. You are supposed to enjoy life. Life is supposed to be great. Go after a great life and try to make other people's lives great and you have opened the first door to purpose.

2. BE ABLE TO COMMUNICATE

Genesis 1:28 states, *"God blessed them and SAID TO THEM..."* God created Adam and Eve, to communicate with them. The Word tells us that God walked with them in the cool of the day. He gave them the ability to talk and listen. They were created with a mouth and a tongue and a language so that communication would be possible. They were created with ears to hear and emotions to feel and connect.

This design shows purpose. You are here to communicate. You are here to listen. That is why Jesus said on so many occasions, "Let him who has ears to hear, hear." You have ears to hear, you have to hear. There are 2 connections we can glean from this design.

A) You are here to communicate with God
I never like the idea that hearing from God is difficult. As a matter of fact, whenever the way seems murky and I am not quite sure which direction the Lord want me to follow, I get

frustrated with myself. Clearly I must be out of range from God's signal. That is why I fast and pray and am faithful in church. I have to stay in a place where I have good reception.

I'm sure you've seen the cell phone commercial when the man continually asks, "can you hear me now?"

That is a question God is asking you. Can you hear Him now? What does He have to do to get your attention? Don't you know that you have a right to expect to hear from God for yourself? This is not Pastor Adam and First Lady Eve, they are just Adam and Eve. There is no church yet, there is no church service yet. They are created and God communicates with them.

So I am suggesting that a part of your purpose is to be in communication with God. It gives a whole new meaning to the pursuit of the spiritual. You shouldn't just seek Him for blessing. You shouldn't just seek His face when you are lost and looking for direction. You should be seeking Him because that is what you were created for. You were created to communicate with God.

B) You are here to communicate with others
It is a common dramatic theme to have a character that wrestles with communication. How many times have you been watching a movie or a show on television and you find yourself screaming at the screen, ok maybe not screaming but saying, "just tell them the truth!" Or, "just speak up" or "tell her that you love her, tell

him that you love him." Whole seasons can be swallowed up by a lack of communication.

We almost accept it as the norm. But that is not how life is supposed to be. You are supposed to be able to communicate. You are here to speak and hear and be heard. That is a part of your purpose.

At the time of this writing my boys were 16. They were just starting to date. Right now, at this moment one of my sons is in a dispute with his "girlfriend." When he asked me for advice I said to him,

"Son, you are 16. This is all about preparation. Is this girl the person you will spend the rest of your life with? Who knows? I doubt it, but who knows. But the key is communication. You are trying to find someone that you can communicate with. Whatever you do, don't start holding back your honesty because communication is a test to see if what you have is real"

So many people are unhappy because they are not communicating. But understand, communication is a part of your purpose. Someone said to me the other day,

"Pastor, you speak so well. This is what you were made for, you were created to talk!" I responded by saying, "we are all created to talk."

It is true, we are all created to speak. All of us have a story to tell, all of us have a word to share. You have to stay open and speak. You cannot let your anger or hurt cause you to turn inward and stop talking to people. You have to speak to your friend, your mother, your mother – in – law, your husband, your boss. Speak up. Tell the truth in love. Communication is a part of your purpose.

3. BE FRUITFUL

Again, in Genesis 1:28, it says, *"God blessed them and said to them, be fruitful and multiply, increase in number; fill the earth and subdue it, rule..."*

I love the attitude that God expects us to have. It is not a shy, timid, just try to get by, attitude. He created us to be kings and queens. He wanted us to be fruitful. You have to understand that this is also a part of your purpose. You are here to reproduce after yourself.

Again, just look at the design. Just as your mouth and ears indicate to you that you are here for communication, your private organs are designed for reproduction. You don't even have to be thinking about reproduction. Adolescence causes your reproductive system to come on line, whether you want it to or not.

Why do you think you were designed this way? It is because God wants fruitfulness always on your mind. And when I say that I don't mean sex. But your sex drive is an indicator of your purpose to reproduce. You should be fighting to be fruitful.

If you have a degree, you should be pushing that degree to bear fruit for you. Your business ought to bear fruit. Your company, your church, your family, your investments, they all ought to be fruitful.

You should be looking for your Eden. You should be looking for the place where fruitfulness comes easy. One of the curses attached to sin was that Adam would produce by the sweat of his brow. As a result of disobedience, fruitfulness got a whole lot tougher. But now that Jesus, the second Adam, has restored what we lost in the garden, we should expect a harvest. If you find that fruitfulness is not happening, you may not have found your Eden.

Your purpose is to push back fear and walk in dominion. Nothing should have rule over you. Men were not created to be ruled by other men. We can be led, but something about rule begins to rub us the wrong way. Slaves dream of freedom because we were created to rule, not to be ruled.

Nothing should have you bound. If you are under the thumb of a habit, then you've lost your purpose. Your purpose is to rule, not be ruled. Be determined that nothing will have you bound. Not cigarettes or not alcohol; not lust of the flesh, not fear and certainly not food.

Your purpose is to fill the earth. You should be reproducing yourself in others. Not just physically, but spiritually as well. You are here to win the lost. Jesus said to go into all the world and preach the gospel. That command wasn't just to me and all of the other men and women of God that you respect. That command was to mankind. As we stated in the last chapter, all of us have a call to win the lost.

Your purpose is to be fruitful. Begin to see winning people to Christ as a part of your purpose. When you seek the kingdom first, all things are added to you. Pushing the growth of the kingdom, that is why you have been allowed to live. You are here to be fruitful.

4. BE FULL

In Genesis 1:29 God says to Adam and Eve,

"I give you every seed-bearing plant on the face of the whole earth and every tree that has fruit with seed in it. They will be yours for food."

Here we have two people being given every plant, every tree and all fruit for food. Obviously God created us to have more than enough. Anyone who has problems with the idea of prosperity just has to read these few verses in Genesis. God started Adam and Eve with more than enough. You have a purpose that is greater than just getting by on barely enough.

Again, we just have to look at the physical design. We were created with a mouth, teeth, a digestive system and an immune system. And there is nothing quite like the feeling of a full belly and a healthy body. God did not create us to be hungry or weak or sick. He created us for health and strength and wholeness.

Exercising, eating right and caring for your temple is a part of your purpose. And you will be surprised how much better life looks when you get the proper rest and exercise.

When we are in the right place, we should have more than enough. I believe that fullness is a part of our purpose. Your bank account should be full, you should have more than enough. You should have more than enough opportunities. You have a right to expect more, more than enough. Pushing for the overflow is a part of your purpose.

When I as a kid, I was always getting into trouble for pouring myself too much juice. First of all, my father hated to spend money. He believed that juice was a luxury in the first place. All we needed to drink was water. And if we did get juice, a sip was enough. "You got to taste it, now go drink some water!" When I was a teenager and got my own job, I used to go buy my own juice just so I could have as much as I wanted.

So when I was a kid, and Dad was not around, and I poured my own juice, I would pour juice until it shimmered right at the top of the glass. I would have to take a small sip just so I could walk with it. No one wants just enough, we all want overflow.

That is what I am believing for You. I want you to rebuke poverty. Understand that lack is not what you were created for. Think about it. If you eat too much, your belly just stretches. You won't pop, you just expand. Your skin has stretch marks because your skin is made to expand.

No limits, no boundaries, I see increase all around me! Who sang that? Israel Houghton? Release me, enlarge my territory! Ask God to enlarge your territory. It is what you were created for! Belly FULL!! Bank Account FULL!!! Opportunities FULL!!!

Every tree is yours for food. Your purpose is to trust God for more!

5. BE USEFUL

The Creation story then picks back up in Genesis chapter 2. In Genesis 2:15 it says, *"15 The Lord God took the man and put him in the Garden of Eden to work it and take care of it."*

Adam was created to work in the garden. We all have work to do. You have a right to work. You are supposed to put your hands to things so that God can bless them. He promised to bless the work of your hands. The only way for that to happen is for your hands to be busy. Work is a right of creation, you are on this planet to be useful. You have to believe that.

To be fulfilled in this purpose you have to find your gift. Everyone has gifts. We can ignore our gifts by being overly focused on other people's gifts. But believe me, you are gifted. People who can't find their gifts aren't looking hard enough and they are not looking in the right place.

Finding Your Gift

A) Teamwork

The beginning of finding your gift is joining a team. You may think you aren't gifted until you join a team. I was watching a bit of the NFL Combine, which is basically the tests they give the players before they are drafted. Everyone is timed for speed in the 40-yard dash, but your result depends on your position. Sometimes I wish there was a Kingdom Combine. You could find that what you do well is very valuable when it is applied to a team. Where one person is faster, the other is stronger. But what we tend to do is judge everyone the same and that is not fair.

If you are feeling like you are worthless, you are definitely not on a team. Join a church, join a ministry, volunteer, give of yourself and you may find the gifts that are hidden within you.

B) Don't always go for the Glamour Positions

Do you remember "Glamour shots?" Have you ever seen someone's picture after they have taken "glamour shots?" They could take the scariest woman and make her look like a super model. I only say woman because I never met a man who went and got Glamour shots done.

Sometimes when we think gifted, we think STAR of the show. We think of the stage and we think of our name in lights when we think gifted. Gifted does not always mean fame. Sometimes the people that are truly gifted in an area make what they do seem so easy that everyone thinks they can do it. But just because it looks easy does not mean it is easy.

Start by serving behind the scenes. Join the team that doesn't get a lot of praise. You will find you have more gifts than you think.

C) Listen to People You Respect

You can't just listen to people you love and especially you can't only listen to the people who love you. People who love you are great, but because they're on your side, they cannot be objective enough to tell you the truth.

I remember when I used to watch American Idol. It was amazing to me how many people would argue with the judges when they told them that they couldn't sing. Just because your mother is in the lobby with her bible clutched to her chest believing that you will be a star, does not mean that you can sing.

Regarding this subject, you have to be very careful. I have had people tell me they respect me and then "lose" respect for me when I tell them the truth. If you really do respect that person, then hold on to that respect. If you are going to find your gift, you need to hear the crowd a bit. If no one thinks you can sing, then maybe you can't sing. Believe me, everyone is not out to get you. It may be that you aren't gifted in that area. But that does not mean that you are not gifted at all.

D) Find what You Like to Do

One of the reasons you want to be led by the spirit is so that you can follow your desires. You need to be able to trust your desires. The Word says in Psalm 37 that if you delight in the Lord then He will give you the desires of your heart. Obviously, taking delight in the Lord, finding joy in His presence is going to change me. A part of the reason God can give me the desires of my heart is that my heart changes. What I desire starts to change.

Trusting what you like can be a path to finding what you do well. There is a work for you to do. God has gifted you and that gift is connected to your purpose.

6. BE AWARE

Genesis 2:16-17

16 And the Lord God commanded the man, "You are free to eat from any tree in the garden; 17 but you must not eat from the tree of the knowledge of good and evil, for when you eat from it you will certainly die."

This creation moment gives us one of the clearest views into the mind and intention of God. The Lord decided to do something that has forever and will forever shape the prospects of the Earth. He introduced CHOICE – FREE WILL. I know there are some that would suggest that God should make all of your decisions for you.

I remember seeing a bumper sticker that said, "God is the Co-Pilot." Then later I saw the same bumper sticker, but now the "co-pilot" was crossed out and the word "THE" was in all caps so that it read, "God is THE pilot."

I remember thinking to myself, "I'm not so sure being THE pilot is what God had in mind when He created us." I know that He is here to lead me, but why would I need to be led if He is going to make all of the choices? Didn't Paul say something about knowing the will of God in Romans?

Romans 12:2 says, *2 "Do not conform to the pattern of this world, but be transformed by the renewing of your mind. Then you will be able to test and approve what God's will is—his good, pleasing and perfect will."*

So that "YOU will be able to test and approve what God's will is," but why would you need to do that if Jesus is the pilot? You wouldn't! In this life, you are going to have to make decisions. You are going to have to make choices. Your purpose is to be aware, to be alert. Your purpose is to watch, pray and consider. You have been given a mind so that you can reason and think while you pray. And although there are some kingdom things that do not make sense and there is a peace that passes understanding, you will still need to use your mind.

To be educated, that is your purpose. To be transformed by the renewing of your mind, to read and to study. Even this moment, reading this book is tapping you into your purpose.

If God wanted to make all of your choices, why introduce this tree. If the tree was off limits, why even mention it, why even put it within reach? That is like telling a 3-year-old not to eat any candy when there is a bowl of it sitting on the desk. At some point it borders on entrapment.

But Gad gave them this choice, and in His infinite wisdom, He introduced free will into the world. We are still living with the results of that decision. People have the power to make choices. You have the power of choice. The fact that you have that power is a glimpse into your purpose. You have to ask for wisdom.

I believe God gave us choice for 2 reasons.

2 Reasons for Choice

A) God is Love

The Word tells us that in 1 John 4, "He that loveth not knoweth not God for God is love." If God is love, then the only way that He can truly receive love from us is if we have a choice. Robots can't love you back. Where would the love be without a choice. God puts the tree there and in essence says, "choose your love for me over this tree." Even now, you have the power to choose Him or reject Him. We all have free will.

B) God wants to Lead

The Lord has put you here to have life and to have it to the full. He wants you to be free and He wants you to seek Him. We all have to resist the temptation to adopt a fatalistic perspective where everything is up to the Lord. Certainly, I am chasing His will for my life. But a part of the journey is to read and study and pray so that when evil comes I can stand my ground.

Your purpose is make choices and to assist others in making the right choices. Counsel is priceless. People need someone to help them to see what the Lord is saying about the next step. In their seeking of the will of God for their lives, He may send them to you.

I was talking to one of my members and she was telling me that everyone is always trying to tell her their problems. She was saying it as a complaint. I felt her pain. Sometimes people in pain can be insensitive to where you are at the moment. She had a life of her own and she had her own problems. I totally understood where she was coming from. But I felt impressed of the Lord to say to her, "perhaps the Lord is leading them to you because you are anointed enough to advise them."
People need counsel. People need a listening ear that then has a godly answer behind it. Making right choices, choosing God over man, this is a part of your purpose. It is why you are here. You shouldn't be surprised when you find yourself in a situation

where you are not sure exactly where to go. You are here to decide. Choose ye this day whom you will serve. As for me and my house, we will serve the Lord.

7. BE CONNECTED

Then finally, Genesis 2:18 states: *18 "The Lord God said, "It is not good for the man to be alone. I will make a helper suitable for him."*

If God said being alone was not good, then you know you were created for connection. You were created for love. That is a part of your purpose. It is a right that you should claim. You have a right to have love in your life. You are not supposed to be by yourself all of the time.

You need people that you can depend on and people need to be able to depend on you. The power of family is extremely potent. I know that we have gotten away from this picture in our current culture, I know that we are determined to redefine family. But I still contend that a strong family produces strong people. I am determined to make strong family a part of my focus. For many of you, strong family is a big part of your purpose.

Let's end this chapter talking about…FAMILY POWER

When I say Family Power I mean:

A) Parents that Provide

I am determined to provide for my children's children. I am trying to leave a legacy. If you had parents that left you nothing but debt, understand that was not the plan of God. Wealth takes more than one lifetime to accumulate.

Providing for my children has become a huge part of my purpose. I have this dream of building each of my children a house. Imagine if you never had to pay for housing, where would you be financially? The work that I am doing is not for me, it is for them.

B) Friends that Always Believe

I want friends that rejoice with me when I am victorious and I want to be that kind of friend. You want to be a friend that loves at all times. You need friends that love you no matter what. That has to be a part of your purpose. In this dog eat dog world, people need to know that there is someone that they can depend on. Friends like that become family.

C) Romance that Leads to Marriage that Lasts

Most of the work I have done has been with love and relationships. I do believe that marriage is God's picture. Marriage covenant is powerful. And although marriage is on the decline in our current world, I still believe it is a foundation to strong family.

You should not be involved romantically for sexual recreation. That is not what love and sex were created for. That is not your purpose. If you are looking for romantic love, you have a right to find it. That purpose lies in finding a life partner. Men need to find a wife and women need to be found by a husband. It is not good for humans to be alone; find the helper suitable for you and experience abundant life.

Congratulations! You have made it past another mountain. I trust you are not just reading. I trust that you are asking the right questions and making notes that speak to your individual situation. This chapter was supposed to get you to ask the question, "what is my purpose?" Don't take another step until you do.

When most people ask, "what is my purpose?" what they are really asking is, "what is my special unique purpose?" But now you know, this is not about fame; this is not about glory. This is about your mission.

I know that you are here for a purpose and now you know that too. Walking in humility, joining a team and being faithful, will connect you to your mission. Until you find your mission, you need to stay right here at this mountain. It will continue to block you (and it should) until you know your purpose. Once you are clear about you purpose, you are closer than ever to the key to greatness and MORE.

You must understand, the enemy will start to get nervous when you start to walk in your purpose. You are becoming a threat to his plan. But let him be nervous, you are being prepared for something you have never imagined. And the best is yet to come. You are called! Chase purpose and find a life full of meaning! Ready? Good! On to the next mountain!

Chapter 5

MOUNTAIN #4
The ATTACK of the Enemy

Ephesians 6:10-12

10 Finally, be strong in the Lord and in his mighty power. 11 Put on the full armor of God, so that you can take your stand against the devil's schemes. 12 For our struggle is not against flesh and blood, but against the rulers, against the authorities, against the powers of this dark world and against the spiritual forces of evil in the heavenly realms.

Be advised, you are getting close to the impossible. Power is becoming more and more available. And the stakes are higher because the rewards are so magnified. There is so much more in store for you and you are about to turn the corner. When you get this close, the devil will try to back you up. And that is the next mountain, the attack of the enemy.

Obviously we can't talk about mountains and not discuss a direct assault from the enemy. He is walking around as a roaring lion seeking whom he may devour. The devil is busy. I am sure we can all agree on that. Although the world may beg to differ, we know the truth. I heard a line in a movie that said, "the greatest trick the devil ever pulled was convincing the world he didn't exist." I think it was "The Usual Suspects."

Quite a trick and sadly, for many people it has worked. The enemy has gotten subtle and changed tactics. He has become more of a crouching tiger than a roaring lion. He is quietly sneaking up on a culture that has decided to ignore him.

But we must be aware of his devices. Paul warns us that our real battle is with the supernatural. At the same time, every challenge is not the devil.

There are 3 beings that should be held accountable for the challenge you are facing.

Who is at Fault in the Challenge?

1. YOU

We have spent quite a bit of time in this book admonishing you to examine yourself so I won't beat the point to death. But we used to sing a song in the old church that said,

"It's me, it's me, it's me, oh Lord standing in the need of prayer. Not my brother, not my sister, but it's me oh Lord, standing in the need of prayer."

When a challenge comes my way, my first question is, "was that my fault?" Before you go rebuking the devil off of your finances, I would suggest that you start with you. Rebuke yourself, cut up your credit cards, get a financial plan together. Is the enemy really keeping you poor, or is it you? The devil didn't buy those shoes, you did. You get the point. Check yourself first, and then you can focus on the devil.

2. GOD

I am not trying to blame God for problems, but He does lead me into situations where I need Him. Even though I walk through the valley of the shadow of death, I fear no evil for He is with me. The truth is, there have been plenty of times where I ended up in that valley following the will of God.

It doesn't make any sense rebuking God if the trouble you are facing is the path to your destiny. You fight Goliath to get a sword for a later battle. I have rebuked plenty of mountains, only to hear the Lord telling me to be quiet. If He has allowed this to happen for His purpose, you have to follow Him. Even Jesus said, "Lord, if it is possible, let this cup pass from me." His trouble was overwhelming, but it was the plan of the Lord to redeem us.

You understand the point. Let no man say when he is tempted that I am tempted by God, for God tempts no one with evil. I hear you, I know the Word. I am just making the point that conflict with the enemy is often God's idea, because He wants the enemy pushed back. He hardened Pharaoh's heart so He could display His power. He incited the Philistines against Samson to cause Samson to destroy them. Some of the greatest strides you have made have happened because God allowed a challenge that made you stronger.

2. The ENEMY – the Devil

I want to spend the rest of this chapter helping you to identify the mountain of the Enemy. How can you know when it is the devil that has attacked you? What form does his attack take? What is a direct attack from the Enemy?

When I was playing basketball in school, one of the things the coaches would do to prepare us to win was to tell us the tendencies of our opponents. If a guy always liked to go left, the coach would tell you that so that you would know how to defend against that guy. We need to be aware of how the Enemy attacks so that we will not be caught off guard.

Most of what the Bible admonishes about the devil is to be aware of him. I love that. I love that the Word does not want you to be worried about the devil, the bible doesn't talk as if the devil has all of this power over you. His power is primarily influential. He does not have authority over you when you are a believer. You just have to be aware of his devices and not give him a foothold.

So let's spend a bit of time breaking down what the devil's attacks look like so we can recognize if this mountain is actually the enemy. To do this we simply have to look at the Word and see how the Bible refers to the devil. Within his titles we find his purpose and his tactics.

The Enemy's Titles and Tactics

A) Thief
John 10:10 "***10** The thief comes only to steal and kill and destroy; I have come that they may have life, and have it to the full.*

Jesus refers to the devil as the THIEF. His tactic is to steal, kill and destroy. When I think about the attack of the enemy, this is the primary passage that comes to mind. He is a thief, a very effective thief. His plan is to use whatever is necessary to rob you, to take from you what is rightfully yours.

He will try to steal from you. He will try to kill you if you give him the chance. One of the reasons I have never tried any illegal drug is because the old mothers in the church warned us against giving the enemy a chance to kill us. They made me believe that the one time I tried it would be the time that there would be a lethal dose. It may not have been exactly accurate, but it kept me from ever trying anything.

I know, if given half a chance and if I stray too far out of the protection of the will of God, the enemy would happily take me off the planet. And he would love to do the same to you. For some of you, that is exactly what you are fighting right now, an attack against your physical body. I am standing with you. Cancer cannot have you. This mountain has to be rebuked, and with God on your side you will live and not die! Death seems to be one of the devil's favorite bombs to lob at us, thankfully death has no sting when you are set free from sin.

The enemy also likes to destroy things. He loves to just wreck stuff, especially relationships. I am more upset with the enemy over ruined relationships than anything else. He loves to widen the differences. You can have 20 things in common and 1 difference and the enemy will so accentuate that difference that you lose the relationship. If he can, he will destroy you and your reputation.

As a man of God, I am so aware of the enemy's plan to destroy my reputation. He knows he can't stop God, so he will settle for ruining your ability to bring people to God. Trust is the currency of ministry. For any pastor or minister that is reading this book, understand, the fight is for your reputation. If he can, the enemy will ruin your reputation even while your gifts are still operating. And there is almost nothing sadder than a preacher that no one wants to hear anymore.

He will destroy your name if he can. I am amazed at how far stars can fall. It is why fame is so deceptive. Once everyone knows your name and knows all of your strengths, it is simply a matter of time before they learn your weaknesses. We all have weaknesses. The enemy loves to accentuate them and make it seem as if you have no strengths. He will destroy if you let him in and that is why we must be aware of him. Keep him out of your house, keep him out of your ministry, keep him out of your marriage. He is a destroyer. Another title the Bible gives the enemy is...

B) Prince of the Power of the Air
Ephesians 2:2 (NKJV) 2 in which you once walked according to the course of this world, according to the prince of the power of the air, the spirit who now works in the sons of disobedience.

Prince of the power of the air, simply means that, not only does the enemy control the airwaves, the media, but he also has control in the thought realm. In other words, the devil has the power to put a thought into your head but you have the power as to whether or not you are going to dwell on that thought. He can also drop an idea into your mind.

I had a teacher in Bible school who said to us that the enemy is like a bird flying over your head. You can't keep birds from flying over your head, but you can keep them from making a nest in your hair. In the same way, you can't keep the enemy from throwing a negative though at you, but you can keep yourself from dwelling on that thought.

That is why the Word admonishes us to put on the "helmet of salvation." You need salvation, you need prayer, you need church, you need worship songs, you need the Word to protect your mind from the mental assault of the enemy. There are many of you that are actually under that assault right now. The enemy is not happy about you reading this book because it will give you the mental fortitude to resist him. Believe me, he wants you to be his punk forever.

Let's break it down...The Mind Attack

Negative Thoughts
You just can't seem to imagine a brighter day. Everything seems negative to you. I like to think of it as if there is a dark haze over everything you see, almost as if you have shades on. The enemy can definitely bombard your mind with negating thoughts.

Questioning who you are

Nothing makes the enemy more excited than trying to get you to doubt yourself. It is what he did to Jesus in the wilderness. He said, "if you are the son of God." The enemy loves to lob "ifs" at us. All the more reason for you to focus on chapter 1 and know who you are!

Visions of defeat

Instead of seeing the victory, the enemy likes to play imaginary scenes of your defeat. I learned that this is often the primary source of stress and anxiety. Understand, your future is fiction right now. The future has yet to come to pass, but the enemy loves to stress us out by getting us to anticipate a future that is yet to be.

Reminding you of past mistakes

The enemy loves to remind you of the mistakes that you have made, in order to talk you out of a blessing you expect. I was in a time of challenge and I was talking to one of the men of God that is over me. At the time, the enemy had me so focused on a mistake I had made. Even now as I am writing this, he is trying to remind me of that mistake right now. He is trying to tell me that it is a waste of my time to write this book and that no one is going to read it because my faults have disqualified me from the prize. My mentor responded by saying to me...if favor is favor, how could you have lost it when you didn't earn it in the first place?"

I am saying that to YOU and ME today. The grace of God and the favor of God is greater than your sin. His love covers us. As long as you are not walking in that sin, it cannot hold you back from the destiny of greatness you have in God. The problem is that the devil is a...

3. LIAR

John 8:44 (NIV) "You belong to your father, the devil, and you want to carry out your father's desires. He was a murderer from the beginning, not holding to the truth, for there is no truth in him. When he lies, he speaks his native language, for he is a liar and the father of lies."

The devil is a great liar. He has been lying from the beginning. He used just enough truth to deceive Eve into eating from the tree. But that is what he does. He knows how to add just enough truth to lead you down a path that is not right for you.
The devil is a liar!

The old saints used to say that all the time. "The devil is a liar"

And they said it in so many ways. They would emphasize different words to give that phrase different meanings.
Sometimes my mother would say, "The devil **IS** a liar!"

My mother used to say that all the time. She said it to mean,

"Oh no you didn't!"

"That will never happen to me!"

"He tried it, but not this time!"

My father emphasized the word liar. "The devil is a **LIAR!**"

It was almost as if he was talking straight to the devil. Although a lot of times he was talking to his car. He had a Ford LTD station wagon. Anyone remember when they were putting fake wood paneling on the side of the car? The "LTD" stood for "limited edition." I think a part of the reason it was a limited edition was because it was always breaking down. My dad would get in that car, try to start it and when it wouldn't start he would yell, "the devil is a LIAR!"

I think this is a phrase you need to keep handy. It is definitely a part of the devil's attack plan. Revelations 12 calls the devil the deceiver of the whole world.

9 The great dragon was hurled down—that ancient serpent called the devil, or Satan, who leads the whole world astray. He was hurled to the earth, and his angels with him.

He is determined to lead the whole world astray. He and his angels are the biggest liars the world has even seen. You should not be surprised when the world talks crazy. They have been deceived by the greatest con artist of them all, Lucifer.

The devil is always talking to you and telling you how you will never make it, how you will never be healed. He continues talking about how you will never amount to anything, how no one will read your book Pastor Andy and how your latter will be less than your former.

Are these the kind of things he is saying to you? Are those the types of thoughts he is lobbing into your head? Then rejoice! Because the devil is a LIAR!!! You must be closer than ever to your breakthrough. You are about to turn a corner, you are on your way to the greatest moment of your life! You are about to get up from that bed and walk again. My book is going to be a best seller. The world is about to sing your songs! Because the devil is a liar!

Say it!

Say it like you mean it. Say it like my mother says it,

"The devil **IS** a liar!"

Say it like my daddy said it to his Ford LTD!

"The devil is a **LIAR!**"

Decide right now that you will never believe his lies again. He lies, but we walk in the truth. God's Word is truth!

4. Tempter

Matthew 4:1-3

Then Jesus was led by the Spirit into the wilderness to be tempted[a] by the devil. 2 After fasting forty days and forty nights, he was hungry. 3 The tempter came to him and said, "If you are the Son of God, tell these stones to become bread."

If the devil tried to tempt Jesus, then you should expect some temptation to come your way. Thankfully, Jesus shows us what to use against the enemy to defeat him, the Word. But temptation is a part of the devil's tactics.

The devil is constantly aware of where you are. Just as God has assigned an angel to guard you, the devil has assigned a fallen angel to keep tabs on you. He is constantly probing at your weakness and trying to get you to fall back into a sin that you have overcome.

One of the worst things about the devil, is that he's always trying to get you back. You broke up with him, but he is still sending cards and flowers. He doesn't want you to be successful, he is determined to knock you off track.

In Matthew 4 we see several variations of temptations.

Satan's Temptations

A) Command these stones to become Bread

In other words, put your physical needs above your spiritual needs. This is the temptation. Jesus is hungry and exploiting that fact, the devil tries to get Jesus to use His power for His own physical advantage. Conversely, Jesus said, "man does not live on bread alone…"

You have to keep in mind that there is more to you than your physical needs. That is easier said than done because your physical needs are loud. When you are hungry, when you are lonely or when you are angry, there is a temptation to ignore the spiritual and focus on your needs of the moment. You have to be careful not to be like Esau and sell your spiritual future for a pot of stew.

B) Throw yourself down and let angels catch you

"Live on the edge, live recklessly; test the grace of God. God will understand and He promised to still forgive you. He has set angels around you to guard you. You can go to the party this one time. God will understand. You are still young, you have plenty of time to live holy."

Any of that sound familiar? It is a common temptation strategy of the enemy. He wants us to put God to the test. He wants us to push the limits of the grace of God and not because God's grace will run out. Thankfully His grace is sufficient. No, the enemy's plan is for you to have to reap the foolishness that you sow. So that even though God's grace covers you, you still end up dealing with and living with the consequences of throwing yourself down from the high place.

C) The World for Worship

Satan shows Jesus the world and offers Him the world for worship. The devil will try to get you to sell out your soul for wealth, for riches, for houses, for land. And when I say sell your soul, I mean turn your back on God and start to chase things.

I have seen it so much. People come, commit to God, but then the cares of this world and the deceitfulness of wealth can choke out the Word and make it unfruitful. You have to decide that you will worship God more than any other thing. Seek Him first and the wealth, the education, the love and the relationship will be added unto you as well. The enemy wants you to sell out the longer consistency of a relationship with God for the short boost of some worldly possession.

Be like Jesus. Resist the devil and he will flee from you. Don't be surprised when temptation comes your way. Be prepared, this is the battle.

5. Flaming arrows

Ephesians 6:16 "16 In addition to all this, take up the shield of faith, with which you can extinguish all the flaming arrows of the evil one."

Have you ever seen a movie where an army shoots flaming arrows? Flaming arrows are not just meant to hit you and set you on fire. The real aim of a flaming arrow is to ignite the ground so that it catches on fire. A flaming arrow is meant to push you back from territory that you have taken.

That is what some of you are experiencing, flaming arrows. You have come so far and you are reaching new heights. The enemy is quite bothered by how far you have come. And your faith, this mountain moving faith, is not meant just to shield you, it is meant to extinguish the attack that would cause you to lose ground.

You will not lose ground! You have come too far to turn back now! I will never go back. The flaming arrows are meant to bombard you and cause you to retreat. Faith doesn't just protect you, faith protects your territory. Faith protects your progress.

You have to realize that flaming arrows means that you are on the front line. The enemy can see you and, in an attempt to push you back, he is shooting flaming arrows at you. This is a key to destiny, a key to mountain moving. You have to realize that the closer you are to the enemy, the closer you are to your goal.

As you approach the place God has always wanted you to be, very often that is where the enemy has set up a stronghold. When you get to Canaan, don't be surprised when you see giants there. The giants are a signal that the territory is worth fighting for. No one finds fertile ground without any inhabitants on it. The flaming arrows mean that you are close. You are closer than ever to the place God has always wanted you to be. I am closer than ever to the place where God will really be able to use me.

WHAT DO YOU DO NOW?

1) Advance! Keep on moving; don't stop now. The flaming arrows are a sign to advance. Now is the time of salvation, today is your day. And as you advance…

2) Keep your shield up high. Work on your most holy faith. Continue to build your faith. I trust that this book is helping you with that. Build up your most holy faith. You can't give up now. The shield of faith will not only block the arrows, but extinguish them.

As you move forward you will see the rest of us and what we need to do is…

3) Lock Faith shields with each other. That is what we are doing right now. I am locking my shield with yours. We are forcefully advancing. From the days of John the Baptist until now the Kingdom is forcefully advancing. We are a part of a move of God. This is not just about you, this is about His kingdom. Together we can push the enemy back. That attack that was meant to intimidate you, I declare it will be the very thing that inspires you to overcome. This mountain is a tough one. I'm so glad you made it through. When the enemy unleashes his attack, it can seem as if the world is going to end. But you just have to remember the truth.

The devil is defeated. Did you know that? Have you read the end of the bible? He knows his days are numbered. I know that it is possible to be shaken by an attack of the enemy. Believe me, I know. I am recovering from an attack right now. As I was writing I got a text with disappointing news. Like you, I am wondering, "when will this attack end?" And like you, I need these words of encouragement. Things have gotten hotter because you are closer to the breakthrough. Hallelujah, you are closer than ever before. When the mountain is the Enemy, you can rejoice. You must really be moving! Now keep moving, don't give up. The same God that brought you this far can get you the rest of the way!

Chapter 6

MOUNTAIN #5
MORE - Greatness

Matthew 18:1-4

1 At that time the disciples came to Jesus and asked, "Who, then, is the greatest in the kingdom of heaven?" 2 He called a little child to him, and placed the child among them. 3 And he said:"Truly I tell you, unless you change and become like little children, you will never enter the kingdom of heaven.
4 Therefore, whoever takes the lowly position of this child is the greatest in the kingdom of heaven.

Look, you made it to MORE to greatness. You crossed those previous 4 mountains and you are here. You have made it to the power of the impossible. I've got good new and then better news. First, the good news. You have come so far and with each victory you have grown in strength. Your knowledge has grown with each chapter, so you are ready for any challenge. You are exactly where you should be.

And then the better news. If there is any mountain where you will feel the actual tangible power of God at your back, it will be this one. Whenever you feel like you are about to fall off the cliff, a wind will give you a push and you will be back on your way up. If there is any mountain to climb it is this one. There is a God built fortress on the top of this mountain; so, keep your head up and your eyes clear, and let's get to climbing.

Be prepared, greatness is probably the biggest mountain of them all. Be aware that the biggest mountains have the highest and hardest climbs. I can honestly say, that of all of these mountains so far, and all of the mountains that we will share, the one that brings the most challenges is GREATNESS.

Yes, I said it. Even more than the attack of the enemy, even more than people. In my experience, the greatest challenges have come as a result of the call to more. Even now, the attack that has come against me and against even my closest friends, has come because we have desired to be used greatly. We have actually decided to get out of the boat and walk on the water, and all of the sudden the wind picks up.

And when you think about it, this is why Jesus made the promise of mountain moving power. He was talking to His disciples. He was talking to people who He was calling to a higher purpose. No one gets "mountain moving power" to just to have it, or just to move someone who doesn't like you very much on your job. This kind of power was promised to people who are about to change the world. You can't help but expect challenges when that is your calling.

And that is your calling. You are a world changer. Even if it is just your personal world and the world of your children, you are fighting for more. Even if it is to lose weight, or to get out of debt, or to start your own business, we are talking mountains of greatness.

And that is how you know this is worth it all. That is when you have to push even harder. As we said earlier, ground that is worth something will have other inhabitants on it. Fertile ground, land flowing with milk and honey, has a tendency to have giants in it.

Think about it. The moment you decide to believe God for the impossible, you are literally asking for challenge. Since faith is the substance of things hoped for, when you start to hope for something, you are setting yourself up for a battle. You can't be surprised when there is resistance. Whatever you have already seen, whatever great thing that God has already done in your life, your victory, feeds your faith and hunger for more.

Have you ever seen anyone who has so much, but still wants more? Do you think to yourself that if you were Bill Gates you would just go somewhere and take a long nap? Why is he still making computers? Why is he still coming up with new products?

I'll tell you why and it is a key to happiness and abundant life that most people are unaware of. Real happiness does not come from vacation. Actually, what makes a vacation a vacation is the break from the work. The real joy in life is the struggle. You can't really see this until you get to this level. Once you have traveled to this leg of the journey, you can begin to recognize this truth.

Now you are ready. You have passed every mountain so far in the book. By now you should...

A. Know who you are
B. Know who is with you and who is against you
C. Understand your purpose
D. Understand and Survive the attack of the Enemy

You have gone through every mountain that we have outlined. And now you are ready for this secret. Ready, here it is...

There is no real life without struggle. There is no MORE without challenge!

Once you get past the struggles that the enemy and life has thrown at you, you have too much strength to go sit on a beach. You gained this faith for a fight.

I remember when I was younger, around 18. My younger brother and I were pretty good basketball players. He was 4 years younger than me and was better than I was. We used to go around to basketball courts in the city of Boston, looking for a game. At this point we were young and in shape. Knees weren't clicking, back wasn't sore, elbows weren't aching. We had the young teenage boy bodies. Remember that body?

When we would go to a court, we would sit there and watch the other guys play for a bit. If there wasn't anyone good at that court, we would get in the car and drive to another court. But if there were some real players there, we would get excited and start to stretch. We would call out, "we got next!" Because when you can really play, you don't want to play with people that aren't good. The whole point of being good is to compete against other people that can test your skills.

Do you get my point? What is the point of being in shape if you aren't going to compete? What is the point of all this power that you have gained, if you aren't now going to put it to work for greatness?

But understand, when you go for greatness there will be a battle. 90% of the stress, at this point in my life, comes from my desire to be a part of something bigger than what I see now. My church is large, but I want more. I have some money, but I want more. My marriage is great, but I want more. Smith Wigglesworth said, "I am satisfied with the satisfaction that is never satisfied."

The German designer Karl Lagerfeld said, "I am never satisfied with myself and that is what keeps me going - I have no post-satisfaction."

There is no post-satisfaction. I love that, don't you? There is no let down after the battle, there are only more battles. Alexander the Great wept because there were no more worlds to conquer. But for you and I, there are still more worlds to conquer. And that is the challenge – greatness, the chase for the eternal.

That is the nature of the passage in Matthew 18. The disciples are asking Jesus about greatness. This is not the only account where this dialog occurs. In a few more chapters, Matthew 22, James and John are after it again. They ask if they can sit at his right hand and left hand in the kingdom.

When you look at either account, I want you to notice that Jesus never rebukes them for the desire for greatness. Actually, I believe that you can't spend time in the presence of God and not begin to expect something great. The longer you are around God and the Word of God and the people of God, the anointing will infect you with a desire for the miraculous. There is greatness in you and there is greatness to achieve.

Let's take a moment and map out the borders of this greatness mountain.

Greatness

1. God's Plan for the World – His Kingdom

Jesus came teaching that the Kingdom of God had come. He taught us to seek first the kingdom, to pray, "thy kingdom come, thy will be done, on earth as it is in heaven." The truth of the matter is that God has big plans for this planet of His. The earth is the Lord's, so He has every right to plan for it.

We all know that the earth is full of trouble. And if we know it, then certainly God knows it. He knows it better than we do since His knowledge is infinite. Whenever someone starts to outline the problems of the world, or even the problem of their country, I often think to myself, "this is why the world needs His Kingdom. God's Kingdom is the answer to it all."

You can't love God and not love what He loves. God loves the world and He loves His answer for the world. And that is why God commands us to pray for His kingdom to come. He wants us passionate about His cure for an ailing society.

The task, to establish God's Kingdom, is a great assignment. And that assignment is a mountain to attain. But it is the mountain of the Lord. But isn't that what the Word promises?

Isaiah 2:2 says...

2 In the last days
the mountain of the Lord's temple will be established
as the highest of the mountains;
it will be exalted above the hills,
and all nations will stream to it.

The mountain of the house of God will be established as the highest of all the mountains. Isn't it so interesting that Isaiah refers to mountains as a place of advantage? I think we may have started this book thinking only of mountains as problems. You probably picked up this book thinking about how to get your problems to move. But as we have gotten deeper, we have seen another truth. The challenge of the mountain brings the blessing of the mountain.

The Prophet Isaiah is saying that God's mountain will be chief among the other mountains. And since this is the Word, and the Word will not return to God empty, but will accomplish what He sent it to do, you can bank on the fact that this will come to pass.

Have you ever been around a bandwagon fan? A bandwagon fan is someone that starts to cheer for a team because the team is getting good and it looks like they are going to win it all. That is what happened to me last year. I started cheering for the Chicago Cubs when they got to the World Series.

In the same way, let's become bandwagon fans for the kingdom. The Lord has the best team; He is going to win the final game. It makes sense to join His team and start playing on His side. And when you start to be about what God is about, there will be a challenge.

Especially since the enemy is God's enemy. There is a supernatural battle that has been going on since the foundation of the world. That war is between darkness and light. You and I are here, in this moment in the 21st century, but this battle started a long time before we got here. And it will be going on long after you and I are gone. Until Jesus returns, this battle will continue.

Like it or not, we are a part of it. Since the enemy knows that God loves the world and the people in it and since the devil can't do anything to God, he tries to hurt God by hurting people. This Kingdom battle is a war of attrition. It is a battle for the hearts and souls of men. You can either be a casualty of this war, or you can pick up a weapon and join the fight.

As for me, and my house, we have decided not to just be meat for the enemy. The best way to be safe from his attack is to be on the offensive. You join the kingdom side. Jesus said that He has come for people to have life, abundant life. He will bring abundant life to you, and even greater than that, He will use you to bring abundant life to other people. There is no greater purpose than that.

2. God's plans for You

One of the most familiar scriptures in the bible is Jeremiah 29:11

11 For I know the plans I have for you," declares the Lord, "plans to prosper you and not to harm you, plans to give you hope and a future.

Not only does God have plans for the world, He also has plans for you. Have you ever wondered why there are so many challenges to face in your own life? It is because when you open your life to the plan God has for you, you start to climb a mountain. One of the amazing things about the mountain of the Lord, is when you climb it, you find blessing for your life.

You do know that God has a plan for you, right? He said to Jeremiah that His plan is to…

A) Prosper you

The word that is translated "prosper" is the Hebrew word "Shalom." It means peace, completeness, health, safety. I will take any of those words and I know that you would too. God's plan is to bring peace and safety as a part of your landscape. This mountain is a fortress. This name of the Lord is a strong tower, you will run in and find safety.

B) Not to Harm you

There may be pain at this level, but that is not the plan of God. When God does allow pain, it is for your good. You have to keep that in mind. This mountain of the impossible, this mountain of power and greatness, there may be some pain up here. The air may get thin, but that is for your good.

I remember when my daughter was first born. When we took her in to get her shots, my wife didn't want to be there, (being a first mothers and all) so I took her. When the nurse was about to give her the shots, she had 4 shots to give her. 2 in each leg. The nurse said to me, "turn her towards you and give her a big hug, with each leg on either side of your lap, and hold her tight."

I remember turning her towards me and as I hugged her, she looked up at me and smiled. A daddy hug, she was so happy. And then...STICK, STICK, STICK, STICK!

I can remember the look of betrayal that came across her face as she started to cry in pain. And I just held her while she cried. I knew it hurt, but it was for her good.

In the same way, sometimes when God holds you the closest, that is when the inoculation is about to happen. STICK, STICK, STICK, STICK and you are looking at God saying, "what is with this pain?" He knows what is best. His plan is to...

C) Give you Hope and a Future

I often have to keep in mind that God knows the end from the beginning. He is the Alpha and the Omega, the beginning and the end. He knows what is to come. His plan for you is not just based on today. His plan is about your tomorrow.

There were so many obstacles that I would have done without, but they were a part of my future. Even some of the difficulty I am currently facing, it is not about today, it is about tomorrow. Wow, I am encouraging myself. Hallelujah, God is in control. And just because you can't see what is beyond this pain, does not mean there is no point to the pain. His plan is for you to end up with more hope.

If you feel hopeless right now, that is not the plan of God for you. You are supposed to find hope in God. Find hope in the fact that He has a plan for you. And hope is an anchor to your soul.

But this is all a part of the process. This is all a part of the chase for great.

3. My Plans for myself

In 1 Samuel 17, when David fights Goliath, there is an interesting exchange that we often overlook in the story. David comes down and hears Goliath's challenge, and that is the part that we love to emphasize.

But in verse 25-26 it says,

"25 Now the Israelites had been saying, "Do you see how this man keeps coming out? He comes out to defy Israel. The king will give great wealth to the man who kills him. He will also give him his daughter in marriage and will exempt his family from taxes in Israel." 26 David asked the men standing near him, "What will be done for the man who kills this Philistine and removes this disgrace from Israel?"

I love this. David fought Goliath, but he didn't do it for free. If David, someone that the Bible calls "a man after God's own heart" can ask, "what do I get?" then so can we. There is nothing wrong with having a plan for your life. Jesus said to seek the kingdom first, not seek the kingdom only. There is a difference and that difference is something we need to be sure about.

Some of us were raised to seek the kingdom only. We sang, "I'd rather have Jesus, more than houses or land. I'd rather have Jesus, more than anything this old world can afford to give"

It was a great hymn, but I was sitting there thinking, "Can I have Jesus and a house? Do I have to be poor to have Jesus? I mean, I'm down to do this whole Jesus thing. What real choice do I have since you are going to make me go to church anyway? But isn't it possible to have both. Nobody here has money?!"

Forgive my teenage brain.

But you get my point. I want to do what Jesus said. He said to seek the kingdom first, and everything else would be added unto you as well. And I don't know about you, but I am looking for the "everything else" that will be added. I have made His kingdom the priority in my life; now I am expecting my harvest.

I know I am not alone. Are you looking for your harvest? Then understand, reaping that harvest is work. That is a part of the challenge of greatness. It took work and faith to sow the seed and it takes work and faith to reap the harvest. Sometimes we act like harvest time is easy time. That is because we don't farm anymore. Harvest time is a time of plenty, but it is also a time of work. Don't be surprised that when you harvest, you'll find yourself exhausted. Thankfully, it is work that is fulfilling.

I absolutely believe you should have high expectations for yourself, but expect some opposition. The obstacle would not be here, if you didn't have great plans. The difficulty was caused by the fact that you dared to have a dream. But don't let that stop you from dreaming and planning. You should want more for yourself. You should have a 5, 10, 15, 20-year plan for your life, and your plan should be great! Your plan should be something that you need faith in God to see come to pass.

4. Greatness for others

At this point in my life, I am thinking so much about my legacy. I want great for my children. You have to realize that you are not just fighting this battle for yourself. You are the pioneer. You are blazing the trail for your children to follow. You are the one pushing back the forest, you are the one making the trails and digging the roads. You are the one laying the foundation that your children and grandchildren will benefit from.

Greatness is not just about you. You have to accomplish something great so that your children will fall in love with success. Even though going for success comes with a risk; your children should gladly take that risk because they watched you step out of the boat.

There is so much greatness that I want for the people connected to me. I want my children to live debt free. I want my children to never have to pay for housing. I want the people that attend my church to become entrepreneurs. I want them to work for themselves. I don't want them to just collect a check, I want them to pay other people to work for them.

I want you to climb this mountain. I want you to be inspired to run your race. God has so much in store for you and I want you to go after it, with all of your heart! I want the world to be a better place because I was in it. I want children in impoverished countries to have a chance at blessing, not just poverty and death. I am believing God for something great! Aren't you?

Of course you are, and that is a mountain!

I want these thoughts to run over and over in your head.

- What am I leaving behind me?
- What will my kids get?
- Did I leave a lasting impression?
- Did I run my race well?

Did you help anyone? Because according to Jesus, that is the price of greatness. If you want to be great, you have to serve everyone. Whoever is the servant, that is the person who is walking in greatness.

HOW DOES THIS HAPPEN?

Good Question, let's finish up this greatness mountain by talking about how to climb it. I just posed a question that is a key to greatness. That question was...

Did I run my race?

We all have a race to run. We all have a battle that lies ahead of us. And at the end, there is a crown. The Lord doesn't want us to just barely slide into heaven by the skin of our teeth. He doesn't want us just missing the tag, like in a close baseball play. Everyone looks at St. Peter and he yells, "safe!" and you say, "whew, I made it. That was a close one. I repented right before that heart attack. Good thing I went to church that Sunday!"

No, God wants you to go after the prize. Paul says in Philippians 3:14: *"I **press** on toward the goal to win the prize for which God has called me heavenward in Christ Jesus."*

God has called you heavenward to gain a prize. You have to go after greatness on this side so that you can hear, "well done, good and faithful servant," on the other side. We all must stand before the judgment seat of Christ. You want to stand there in confidence because in this world you are like Jesus.

So let's get to the question. How do you reach your prize? How do you cross the Greatness Mountain?

That answer is found in Hebrews 12:1-3, 7
12 Therefore, since we are surrounded by such a great cloud of witnesses, let us throw off everything that hinders and the sin that so easily entangles. And let us run with perseverance the race marked out for us, 2 fixing our eyes on Jesus, the pioneer and perfecter of faith. For the joy set before him he endured the cross, scorning its shame, and sat down at the right hand of the throne of God. 3 Consider him who endured such opposition from sinners, so that you will not grow weary and lose heart.

God Disciplines His Children

7 Endure hardship as discipline; God is treating you as his children. For what children are not disciplined by their father?

Running the Race

I want you to see the greatness mountain as a race. You are on the starting line and it's time to get moving. And since from the beginning, we have been saying that this book is for movers, the analogy fits perfectly.

If you are going to accomplish something great, you are going to have to take the steps that are outlined in this passage.

1. See the Crowd

You must realize that you are being watched. The fact that the stands are full should motivate you at an even greater level. You should play well when the game is a big game. And this is your life, this is His kingdom, there is no bigger stage than this. There are 2 crowds that are watching…

A) Heaven is watching

Every other faith walker in heaven is on your side. You are surrounded by a great cloud of witnesses. The word cloud implies that they are above you. The roll call of faith has just been given in Hebrews 11. Clearly chapter 12 is referring to them.

So you should know, you are not alone. You are not the first person to walk by faith. You are not the first person to fight a giant. Keep that in mind whenever you feel your nerve starting to slip. One of the tactics of the enemy is to try to make you feel as if you are unique in this battle. But you are not alone. Moses is watching, David is watching, Paul is watching, Mary and Peter and John and Philip, Elijah and Elisha, they are all watching. And they are yelling, run on!

B) Earth is watching

Your children are watching, your family is watching. People who work with you, people who attend church with you, they are all watching you run your race. Your victory will inspire them.

Whenever I feel like giving up, I feel the eyes that are on me. When I win, I show others how to win. When you win, you show others that greatness is possible. Your victory will blaze a trail for others to follow. This should give you confidence. The Lord needs your example of His power in a person. You are His poster child for faith.

2. Run with Perseverance

The "greatness" mountain is not a sprint, it is a marathon. It is not about quick success, it is about sustained success. We are often impressed with speed and I get that. Usain Bolt is an amazing talent. He is probably one of the greatest sprinters of all time. But I am more impressed with the marathon runners. The ability to maintain a level of speed for 26.2 miles, now, that is amazing!

To maintain endurance, you have to run light. You can't carry people that you have never forgiven on your back. They are too heavy, you will never make it. You can't allow sin to entangle your legs and trip you up. You are going to have to make sure your life is clean. We have seen so many powerful men and women of God start so strong and then sin causes them to fall. We have to learn from their mistakes and keep our legs clear.

I love the fact that the writer encourages us to run that way, to run with endurance. So much of greatness happens as a result of endurance. Being a great mother is not just what you do in the first 5 years. That is a great start, but to be a great mother, you have to maintain your pace. Great marriage, maintain that pace, great church, maintain the pace, great company, maintain the quality. There is nothing worse than a quick start and a poor finish.

I grew up in Boston watching the Boston marathon every year. I used to think, "I wish I could get a number and get up front and sprint out into the lead for the first 2 miles. The news would be saying, 'Who is this Andy Thompson guy?' And I would be famous for about 2 miles."

There are many problems with my plan, but the main problem is that I would never be able to maintain that pace. And this is what happens to people in life. We try to run with speed instead of running with consistent strength. To ascend the mountain of greatness, you will have to keep at it. Keep chopping at that tree, it will come down.

3. Run Your Race

The Word says to "run with perseverance the race marked out for us." You have to run the race marked out for you. I want you to see this in 2 ways...

A) This is a relay race

Jesus is the author and the perfecter. He started in the blocks at Calvary and He will run the anchor leg of this race. He handed the baton of faith off to His disciples and faith has now been passed into your hands. And right now, in this moment, you have to run your leg of this race. You have to ask yourself, "did I leave faith better off than when I found it?"

For those of us who are younger than the Baby Boomer Generation, we have our work cut out for us. They have set a torrid pace for us and now we have to make our move and run our race.

B) Run YOUR race

You can't look at other people. You ultimately are running against yourself. You are just trying to reach your own potential. One of the biggest mistakes we can make (and I am sure we made this point in the "People Mountain chapter") is to compare ourselves to other people. Don't worry about what everyone else is doing. You run YOUR best race.

4. See Properly

When you are in a relay race, you look back long enough to know that the baton is in your hand. After that, you have to keep your eyes trained forward. You have to focus on Jesus for 2 reasons…

A) He is the Example

When you see how Jesus ran, then you will know how to run. He didn't just come to die for us, He came to show us how to live. He came to show us how to run this race toward the prize. When you see what Jesus had to endure, it should inspire you to keep running. You haven't shed blood yet.

B) He is the Finisher

His grace is sufficient. No matter who you are, you will fall short in some area. When you decide to step towards greatness, you have to acknowledge that you are going to need help. If perfection was required for a miracle then we are all in big trouble. None of us are perfect.

Thankfully, you are not running alone. You are on a track team. This is a relay race. Run the best leg of this race that you can and then let the Lord do the rest. You do your part and let God do His part.

5) See Hardship as Discipline

My sons play basketball. I was at one of their practices the other day and when they made a mistake, the coach made them run sprints. When the practice was over and they were back in the car, one of them said to me, "this coach has such an anger problem. He gets so mad at us for the smallest thing and then makes us run."

My response to him is my response to you. I said, "he isn't making you run because he is mad. He is making you run to get you in shape. He is just using your mistakes as an excuse. Realize, practice is to get you in shape!"

You have to endure difficulty as if God is making you run sprints. He is treating you as sons. You know you are His child because He trusts you to go through challenges. The more sprints you run, the better shape you will be in. You are stretching your endurance with each sprint. With each challenge, you are getting prepared for the great thing that God wants to do in you and through you.

Do you see it? Do you hear it – that call to greatness? Look at this mountain. It is high, it is full of challenges, but that is the point of this power. You receive power to walk consistently in power. You are now equipped with the knowledge to accomplish something great. I am so proud of the progress we are making. Remember, greatness is our aim. Now that you are here, we need to lay the foundation to stay here. It's time to build a fortress.

SECTION 2

BUILDING THE FORTRESS

Congratulations on the work that you have done to move through this mountain range. Some of the mountains, like negative people and the attack from the enemy, you had to speak to and rebuke. Some of them you had to tunnel through. We started off tunneling, digging deep into ourselves and finding the gold mine that is your strength in Christ. You had to dig deep to find your purpose and you now have a well deep within. I encourage you to go back and access those notes, you can use those tunnels in the future to make progress.

You have also done some climbing. You realized that mountains are going to be a part of your landscape. Mountains aren't all bad. You moved it by redefining it and you climbed the mountain of greatness. The strength you gained was always about reaching for great, achieving something awesome. The goal was always for you to believe God for something that you could not see. The chase was always for something that your eyes had not seen and your ears had not heard, something your mind had never conceived. And now that you are here, you have to stay here.

It's time to build a fortress. To build the fortress properly, you need to have an idea of what you are keeping out. I want to focus on the 3 things that I believe can knock you down from the power you are walking in. A fortress has four walls, and each wall we build will be designed to keep out the infection that would try to cause you to rot from within.

With that in mind, we will spend the rest of the book focusing on building these 4 walls.

1. Wall against DOUBT
2. Wall against FLESH
3. Wall against LAZINESS
4. Wall against TIME

Jesus is called the stone that the builder rejected. You are a mover, now let's focus on building. You do not want to fall from this mountain. God has so much for you to do. He has such a plan to use you. So much will be added, if you can just hold on. You can do it! Hold on! Be ready to defend the faith that you have acquired. Get these walls up quickly.

Chapter 7

The DOUBT Wall

Mark 9:21-24

21 Jesus asked the boy's father, "How long has he been like this?" "From childhood," he answered. 22 "It has often thrown him into fire or water to kill him. But if you can do anything, take pity on us and help us." 23 "'If you can'?" said Jesus. "Everything is possible for one who believes." 24 Immediately the boy's father exclaimed, "I do believe; help me overcome my unbelief!"

One of the biggest enemies to faith is not doubt, it is the inability to admit that doubt exists. That is one of the few things that was missing in my faith education, but I am determined it will not be missing as I teach faith.

Hear me, doubt is a factor in faith. Even when you are standing in absolute total confidence, you know that you are there because you have overcome your doubt. You are still aware of doubt and you are aware that your doubts have gone silent.

But right in the middle of belief is unbelief. Doubt and fear will always be a factor on the greatness mountain. Anyone who never deals with fear or doubt isn't on this mountain with us. When you decide to do something great for God, or something great for your family, believe me, doubt tries to invade. Fear and doubt can be loud. And you will measure your success by the fear and doubts that you have overcome.

That is why I love this passage in Mark 9, especially verse 24. I love the response of this father. He says, *"I do believe; help me overcome my unbelief!"* Can you relate to that? He states the overwhelming situation that is great faith. That situation is…

Belief vs. Unbelief

Especially when you start to look for a miracle. Is that you? Are you looking for a miracle? Are you expecting something that seems impossible? There is a difference in needing a miracle and looking for a miracle. You can need a miracle but never expect one. When you start to expect a miracle, fear and doubt try to creep in. I do believe; help me overcome my unbelief! Let me translate that for you. In other words, what he is saying is...

Faith is not my problem; my problem is unbelief.

We all have been given a measure of faith. All of us have faith. Jesus said faith the size of a mustard seed was enough. So even if you are sitting here thinking your faith is small, understand, small faith is not the problem. The problem is big doubts.

Having big doubts can still happen on the mountain of greatness and that's why we are building this wall of this fortress. What you are looking for is so unbelievable, that sometimes, the sheer unbelievable-ness of it tries to overwhelm the belief you have.

So let's take a closer look at this story. By doing that we can see the source of this father's unbelief and the source of our unbelief as well. By focusing on the source of the doubt, we can address it at the source and do a better job of defending against it. But just keep this in mind, you don't build a fortress for a one-time battle.

You build a fortress because you are in hostile territory. This wall has to be built and maintained, because you don't defeat doubt once. Doubt is in your area. It likes to hang around greatness. I don't even attribute doubt to the devil anymore. My doubts are caused by the sheer magnitude of my belief. I think of the doubt as the shadow cast by the sun of my faith. And the bigger the project, the bigger the doubts seem.

The Source of the Doubt

1. The Sheer Magnitude of the Miracle

I just made this point, so I won't restate it. The father was looking for his son to be healed from something life threatening. This wasn't a cold, this wasn't a sore throat. This was a problem that could not be solved without Jesus.

Problems that require Jesus are awesome, since Jesus has the power and the will to help us. But for "anything" to be possible, faith has to overwhelm doubt.

2. A Demonic Attack

I would contend that direct assaults from the devil can be particularly frightening. And when you are afraid, it can be hard to locate your faith. When you are on Greatness Mountain, the devil will attack you. Just know that this is an even greater sign that God is for you. When God's enemy shows up, you know that God must be around.

In this particular story, the spirit is described as having the ability to affect hearing and speech. I can't help but see a connection for you and I. Nothing would make the enemy happier than to rob you of your ability to hear the Word and speak the Word. Faith comes by hearing and faith is activated by what you say. I am sure even when you have been reading and studying this book there have been multiple distractions. The enemy does not want you to gain this knowledge and power. But you are winning. Let's keep building!

The attack tries to stop you from praising God. It tries to stop you from testifying about the amazing thing that God has done and what He is about to do.

The spirit also tries to kill the boy. It also caused him to foam at the mouth and roll around on the ground. In essence, to make him look like he is crazy. I know this is blessing someone right now. The enemy is trying to kill you, we knew that. But he is also trying to make you look crazy. He is trying to make every believer look crazy. The world thinks that we are out of our minds. And they are right. I have gotten out of my mind and into the Spirit. You are learning how to "lose that old mind you had" and walk in kingdom thinking.

The spirit also makes the boy go rigid. The attack can be one that tries to make it difficult for you to change. So many believers battle this spirit. Keep in mind, you must remain flexible. True strength is not seen in rigidity, it is found in flexibility. You cannot allow the devil to make you stiff and rigid, hard to be around, awkward and off putting. You need to like Paul, able to be all things to all men so that you might win them.

The attack is a significant factor in the presence of doubt.

3. This is Not Your First Time in Faith

The father says that this is not the first time he has sought a miracle. He went to the disciples first, and nothing happened.

I can hear many of you saying, "Exactly! This is not my 1st time praying for a Miracle. I have been disappointed in the past!"

Believe me, I know. Nothing can cause doubt like failure. But the answer to that is persistence. Jesus asks in Luke 18, "will faith be found in the earth?" Can anyone ask more than once? How many times will you knock on the door? Failure is often the prelude to success. I say keep knocking. Believe me, God is home.

4. The Unbelieving Generation

Jesus calls the generation "unbelieving." I know what you are thinking. "If biblical people were unbelieving, we are in trouble today!" I couldn't agree more. Their world had so much less technology than we do today. They had to have more faith. Even people that weren't Christians were trying to worship something, Baal, or something.

Jesus makes the point and shows us another factor in our doubt. That factor is the time we live in and the people we allow around us. In this story, when Jesus shows up, there is an argument happening. This boy needs healing and the miracle service has turned into a debate. You have to fight against the doubts in this world. You have to battle against the general overall doubt in God that exists in our day.

Have you ever heard a testimony of a miracle and the doubt of our world tries to creep in and make you doubt? We all have to fight this. God can do anything but fail. The supernatural does exist. We all have to hold on to our faith in a world where faith is not popular.

5. The Reaction in the Face of Breakthrough

Something so interesting happens when Jesus is about to heal this little boy. Right at that moment, the symptoms decide to show up. I find this fascinating and edifying, don't you? It would seem to me that the spirit would just lay quiet so that it wouldn't be cast out.

Has that ever happened to you in life? Your car is making a weird noise until you get it to the mechanic. Your knee is hurting, until you get to the doctor. Your computer won't turn on, until you get it to the apple store. Amazing how life is sometimes.

But not in this scenario and I am so glad for that. Once Jesus gets there, the situation goes crazy. It is like the enemy was trying one last push to make the father doubt. And it almost worked. The father actually says "If" to Jesus.

This is a sign to you and me. Let's allow this to be a serious nail in the coffin of doubt. If your situation is acting up right now, if things have gotten even hotter and if the challenge has gotten even worse, then you must be closer than ever to deliverance. Obviously, Jesus must be near. You are closer than ever. Can I say that again? YOU ARE CLOSER THAN EVER! Say that,

"I AM CLOSER THAN EVER!"

Now is the time of your salvation, today is the day. The devil is a liar and he is trying to escalate the situation to make you back off of your dream. But remember, you are on the mountain of greatness. You have come too far to turn back now. Don't let doubt push you back; you push doubt back.

6. The History

Jesus asks him how long the boy has been like this. Time can be a factor. When something has been around for a while, we tend to think that it will be tougher to get over. When you deal with a problem for a long time, doubt really likes to sing loud.

You have to overcome the past. No matter how long this has been an issue, since the Lord is here, since you have entered the greatness arena, change can happen in a moment.

It is so interesting how "taking a long time" tries to fight "gone in a second." Believe me, "gone in a second" is so powerful, that it can even erase the pain of the wait. We are going to talk about

"Time" in the last chapter, the "TIME wall." The fact that this is not new and the fact that this has been going on for a while, has nothing to do with the fact that it is time for it to move. Don't let one time affect the other. Still Believe!

7. The Word "IF"

This father came close to missing his miracle. He said a bad word, the word "IF." Did you get in trouble for saying bad words? I wasn't allowed to say the word "what" to my mother. I had to say, "Yes" or "Yes Ma'am." My parents were so strict. My brother got his mouth rinsed out with soap and he didn't even say a curse word.

I trust that you are free from cussing. Here is a new cuss word for you to avoid. The word "IF." Erasing this word from your vocabulary may be easier said than done, but you must do it. When I am talking about this book, it is easier to say, "if this book becomes a best seller" than, "when this book becomes a best seller." The word "IF" just sounds safer. But "IF' can be a word that triggers doubt.

As best you can, try to keep "IF" out of your mouth when you are talking about your miracle. The words "IF" and "Can't" are words we don't like to hear up here on Greatness Mountain!

Now that we have identified the source of doubt, let's spend the last few moments talking about the tools you need to defeat it.

How do I Overcome Doubt and Unbelief?

1. HONESTY

We said this from the beginning, but it bears repeating. Doubt has the most power when it is ignored. We must focus on it and put it under a microscope so that we can admit that it is there.

To win you have to face the situation. You will never stay on this mountain if you run from the fight. Fight the good fight of the faith. A fortress is a place where soldiers live. You are a soldier and you appreciate peace, but you are not afraid of a fight!

You have to do everything within your power not to get caught in church fakeness. People like to come to church and put on a mask like everything is ok. I have heard people say, "fake it, 'til you make it." And as much as I understand keeping a game face and not crying over every setback, you can't lie to yourself. You can't fake yourself out. If doubt is trying to get in, admit it. This is where good friends come in handy.

You need people on your side who can pray when your doubts get too loud. You can do the same for them when they are in the same situation. Without prayer partners and friends with faith, you won't stay on this mountain of greatness very long. I know the Word says to encourage yourself and you can. But too much time alone can make you vulnerable. Make sure you know who is on your side!

2. Get some Word to Stand on

Faith comes by hearing the Word and faith stays as a result of the Word. When you tell me what you are believing for, you ought to be able to tell me the scripture you are using as a foundation. In case you don't know where to begin, let me give you a few.

A) God is a Giver
James 1:5
5 If any of you lacks wisdom, you should ask God, who gives generously to all without finding fault, and it will be given to you.

Matthew 7:7-8
7 "Ask and it will be given to you; seek and you will find; knock and the door will be opened to you. 8 For everyone who asks receives; the one who seeks finds; and to the one who knocks, the door will be opened.

God is a giver. Did you ever get a "hook up?" A "hook up" is basically another word for "favor." When I was a teenager, 2 of my best friends worked at a McDonalds in downtown Boston. I always went there and took my little girlfriends there because my boys would give me a "hook up."

I would look to see if they were working and then when I saw them, I would give them the "Hook me up nod." As a result, they would give me extra nuggets or extra fries and maybe even throw an apple pie in the bag. Thank God for "the hook up!"

I want you to go to the Mc-Kingdom and look in to see Jesus is always working. Meet His eye and give Him the "hook me up nod" and expect your miracle. Our God is a giver!

B) God is not counting sins
2 Corinthians 5:19
19 *that God was reconciling the world to himself in Christ, not counting people's sins against them. And he has committed to us the message of reconciliation.*

God is not counting your sins against you!

This is a powerful truth to keep in mind. Doubt loves to rest in regret. Your mistakes love to creep up on your mind. The enemy loves to remind you of your past to try to cause you to doubt that God will keep His promises. We never doubt that God can do it. That is not how the enemy attacks us. He tries to get us to doubt that God will.

Thanks be to God that your sins are covered. We have been reconciled to God through Jesus. Your past has been erased. Once you ask God to forgive you, He "remembers your sin no more." You have been justified. It is "just as if I'd" never sinned. That is a good way to think of the word justified. Fear not, you are redeemed. God is not counting your sins against you.

C) God has already said "YES"
2 Corinthians 1: 20

20 *For no matter how many promises God has made, they are "Yes" in Christ. And so, through him the "Amen" is spoken by us to the glory of God.*

God has already said "YES". You don't have to keep asking. You don't have to worry if it will come to pass. You don't have to go to another meeting to hear the answer. The answer is YES, God will move.

The thing about your "YES" is that it is locked in time. You have to keep walking until you get to it. That is why you have to keep saying "AMEN." Amen means "so let it be." Amen is an agreement word. It is the way to keep consistent on your way to better.

3. Get close to Jesus

The father in this story received his miracle for his son, because he got near Jesus. People were always coming to Jesus and receiving something miraculous. We have to take their hint. The answer is to get close to Him.

We have to be careful to make sure that we keep Jesus at the center of our religious practice. I am not trying to cast dispersions on religion. You need a custom that involves religious practice. The Word says in Luke 4, that Jesus went into the synagogue, "as was His custom." If Jesus had a religious custom, then so should all of us. Consistent religious practice is a good thing.

We must keep Jesus at the center of it. Church has to be a way to better develop that personal relationship with Jesus. To keep doubt at bay, you have to stay close to Jesus. We are building this fortress against doubt and Jesus has to be the cornerstone and the king on the throne.

The fortress needs to be a place devoted to prayer. The fortress should be a place where praise is common. There should be consistent Godly fellowship in the fortress. This is how you stay close to Christ. Remember, doubt can get loud, until Jesus shows up.

4. Understand the Belief is the Victory

1 John 5:4

4 for everyone born of God overcomes the world. This is the victory that has overcome the world, even our faith.

One of the greatest revelations you can have on faith is that faith is what the battle is about. The Enemy isn't just after your money, he is trying to rob you of your faith. He doesn't just want to ruin your marriage, he wants to ruin your faith. The fight is not just a fight OF faith, it is a fight FOR faith. This challenge is all about your faith.

I trust we have made that point clear. You have fought to stand on this mountain at this moment. This whole journey was about you growing in confidence in the impossible being possible.

Greatness isn't a mountain to move away, it is a mountain you move to, you live there.

When you understand that, you then realize that the real victory is the faith. The money, that is not the victory. The marriage, the success, the house, the ministry, the children, whatever you are believing for, whatever is your miracle, that is not the victory. It is great and amazing to walk in the manifestation of the promise and when your promise comes to pass, you will still need your faith.

The real victory is the faith. The real victory is in the fact that you went through the challenge and still believed God. Before the battle, you may have wondered if you would worship God no matter what. When I read about Job, I always wonder,

"do I have a limit? Is there a line God can cross that will cause me to walk away from Him?"

I thought that there might be, until I started living. I realized that the tough days and the difficulties didn't push me away from God, they caused me to depend on Him in an even greater way. And I'm still standing. Look! Look at you! You are still standing. You are still reading about faith.

That is what it means to win. When you truly embrace the power of the impossible, you will come to the conclusion that you are going to die believing God for something that has yet to come to pass. That is the nature of faith. The thing that is seen is temporary; the unseen thing is eternal. Once something becomes seen, you start to look for the unseen thing. That is faith. Faith always wants more.

Meaning, when you die, when you go on to your reward in heaven, there will some things in the earth that you never got to accomplish. You simply ran out of time, but you never ran out of faith. And that is what it means to win. You never lose faith, you always believe. No matter what comes my way, I still believe!

Doubt will try to creep in, always. The times I have walked in a faith where doubt never spoke, those times are few and far between. And now, I am developing what I think of as a "doubt callus." Doubt is a factor in faith. Now that we have established this wall, this barrier against doubt, you can stand securely against it. Never let doubt block your miracle! Just remember what Jesus said, "if you can just believe, anything is possible if you can believe!"

Chapter 8

$\leftarrow$————————————$\rightarrow$

The FLESH Wall

Romans 7:15-16

15 I do not understand what I do. For what I want to do I do not do, but what I hate I do. 16 And if I do what I do not want to do, I agree that the law is good. 17 As it is, it is no longer I myself who do it, but it is sin living in me.

There is always a battle. Even during a time of peace, even when you may not have anything specific at that moment to believe

God for, there is still always a struggle. We always have a reason to be on the alert. We can never let our guard down, because even when the enemy is not attacking, there is a battle with your flesh. This is one of the ways that we defined faith in the very beginning of the book. Do you remember? We asked the question...

What does it mean to walk by faith? And the first answer was... To NOT be ruled by the flesh.

It sounds like a very basic answer and I will stop proclaiming it when Christians master it – which means I will never stop proclaiming it. To be ruled more by your spirit than your flesh, that is easier said than done. To walk by faith and not by the flesh means...

A) To not be ruled by your physical senses
Have you ever tried to fast? Have you ever tried to stop eating and just drink water for a day? You get a chance to see how loud your flesh can get. By the second day you are dreaming about food that you don't even like. You have to stop watching TV because there are too many food commercials.

They tell you that "you belong at Applebee's" and you believe them. You want to hurry down to the Olive Garden, where they "Treat you like Family." Subway says to "Eat Fresh" and you want to race down and dive over the glass and make your own super sub of everything. Your flesh is loud.

We all get hot. Your body starts to sweat. You could have just been in air-conditioned space. You step outside for 2 minutes into 100-degree weather and your flesh reacts immediately. Too cold? Same response, your flesh reacts right away. You were just warm in the bed but the minute you step one foot out of the covers, your body reacts. Need another example?

Have you ever smelled something bad? It is so difficult to control your face. It is so tough not to exclaim, "what is that smell?!" It is how your body is designed. You get hungry and you say, "I am starving. I am about to die!" You are nowhere near dying. Most Americans have enough extra weight to last for weeks. But your flesh is programmed to react. To ignore your flesh takes strength.

So when I say…"For we walk by faith and not by sight!"

I want you to change the word "sight" a few times.

"For we walk by faith and not by _____"

Smell, temperature, hunger, thirst, exhaustion – which one do you want to apply? They are tough and all a part of the battle with the flesh.

When I say that you should not be ruled by your flesh, I also mean…

B) *Not Ruled by Your Emotions*

You have to be careful how you react when you are angry. Anger is an emotion that we seem to think is a trump card for behavior. We do something that is unacceptable and our response is, "I was mad. Sorry I ran over your cat, but I was mad. Sorry I keyed your car, but I was angry. Sorry I told you that your feet smell better than your breath, but I was angry. Sorry I told your mother that her chicken was so dry that it gave me strep throat, but I was angry!"

Just because you are angry, does not excuse rude behavior. But we make bad decisions based on emotions. Not only do you need to be careful when you are angry, you need to be careful when you are too happy. Before you go and tattoo "Lucinda" across your back, you need to make sure "Lucinda" is still going to be here in 10 years. Before you tattoo "Grayson" across your butt cheeks, I would suggest you think for a moment. Is Grayson going to be here in 20 years? Even when you are happy, you need to be careful.

You don't want to let your emotions rule you. Don't make major decisions when you are down. If you are having a tough day, that is not the time to make life and death decisions. The aim is to be ruled by faith, not by flesh.

And therein lies the constant battle. It is what Paul is talking about in Romans 7. He is talking about the battle that is Flesh. We often think about this as a struggle with sin, but sin is simply disobedience in some area in your flesh. Ultimately, sin is allowing the flesh to rule.

In order to stay on this mountain of greatness, you can't let that happen, ever! You didn't get here by being fleshly, you won't stay here by being fleshly. When the flesh rises up, you have to be prepared to put the flesh back in its place. Now, don't get me wrong, the flesh does have its place. Everything is not spiritual. But we need to know when to let the flesh be the flesh and when to allow the spirit, and especially God's Spirit, to have His way.

You understand right? Your honeymoon is not necessarily supposed to be a spiritual time. This is where we can miss it in the church. We just overly spiritualize everything and miss the balance that is life.

The fact that Paul talks so openly about the flesh and the potential struggle that can occur with the flesh, allows us this moment to be honest and real. We are on our way to heaven, but we are not there yet. So we need to clearly identify the flesh battle so that we can get this wall up to defend destiny from the attack of the flesh.

Paul breaks the struggle down into these few basic concepts...

1. The Spiritual vs. the Unspiritual
Paul says in Romans 7:14 *"We know that the law is spiritual; but*

I am unspiritual, sold as a slave to sin."

Although the Word is spiritual, you are not always spiritual. Church service and prayer and worship and praise are all spiritual, but you are not always spiritual. What the Word commands you to do requires spirituality, but you are not always spiritual.

Paul is talking about real life. I love this. It happens so rarely in church, where we let our guards down and get honest. He is talking about the Spiritual Word vs. Unspiritual thinking. I have to hide the Word in my heart to override the evil thoughts that continually try to plague me.

Paul is talking about, the Spiritual Church Service vs. Unspiritual Workplace. You are in church with believers on Sunday and at work with unbelievers on Monday. You are in this world but not of the world and that balance is a struggle.

2. I Do Things that Make No Sense
Romans 7:15
"I do not understand what I do. For what I want to do I do not do, but what I hate I do."

Have you ever taken a hard look at yourself? Have you ever thought about the insanity that can be human desire? You want to make money, but you don't want to go to work. You want to have a 6-pack, but you also want to eat ice cream in the bed at night. You want to be married, but you still want to hang out all night with single friends. You want great children, but you want the TV to raise them.

We all do things that make no sense. Paul says, in essence, "what am I doing?! Even I don't understand what I do!"

The things I want to do, have a tendency to be the toughest thing to do. Right now, as I am writing, I should be upstairs working out. This is my workout time. Working out is good for my heart, it is good for my body, it is good for my stress levels but I don't feel like going up there to working out. Am I alone?

I just want to sit here in this chair, and continue our conversation. It is 6:38 pm, I should be getting ready to have dinner, but my wife is out of town. And I have a King-Sized Kit-Kat in the table drawer next to this seat. I am trying to figure out how many calories that is and whether or not that would be a good dinner. If my wife was here I know what she would say, but she is not here! And that Kit-Kat is calling me. I hate that I want to eat it, but I want to eat it.

3. The Fact that I Hate What I do is a Sign that the Word is in Me

Paul continues, Romans 7:16 *"And if I do what I do not want to do, I agree that the law is good."*

The fact that this process bothers me is how I know that I know

187

better. When your own heart convicts you, you know that Jesus is in your heart. The mistakes I made, they really taught me that I was saved. When you can do evil and just sleep like a baby at night, you need to check your spiritual birth certificate. When you can be saved when no one is watching, that is when you know you have crossed from death to life.

When you are really crazy you don't know you are crazy. When you stop and ask the question, "am I crazy?" Chances are, you are not crazy. When you stop and ask, "was I wrong?" That is a sign that your conscience is not seared. You can still sense the convicting power of His Spirit. Paul is saying that the struggle shows that you agree with the bible.

Then he sums the struggle up for us in the final verses...

Romans 7:24-25
24 What a wretched man I am! Who will rescue me from this body that is subject to death? 25 Thanks be to God, who delivers me through Jesus Christ our Lord!

We need help with the flesh. This battle is here to stay. We need the Spirit. We need Spiritual Power to make it. Just when you think the flesh is under control, it tries to rise again. How can we defend against the destructive power of the FLESH? Let's finish up by answering that question. To do that, I want us to look at another passage of Paul's. This one is found in Ephesians 4.

HOW DO WE BUILD THE WALL TO HANDLE THE FLESH?

Ephesians 4:20-24

20 That, however, is not the way of life you learned 21 when you heard about Christ and were taught in him in accordance with the truth that is in Jesus. 22 You were taught, with regard to your former way of life, to put off your old self, which is being corrupted by its deceitful desires; 23 to be made new in the attitude of your minds; 24 and to put on the new self, created to be like God in true righteousness and holiness.

Paul lays it out very plainly, what I will term… Steps to Flesh Control

Step 1 – Submit to Teaching

That is what is happening right now. That is why I am trying to write this as simply for you as possible. I didn't mean for this to be a workbook, but if that is what it is becoming, praise God. Let's get to work. We have a mountain to defend, we have destiny to achieve. Greatness awaits, let's build the fortress!

Unfortunately, people can be more interested in inspiration than instruction. I understand that. I love to be inspired as well. But there is such value in being taught. You cannot just exist on the bread you think you need. You need a word from the Lord and the topic of that word can't always be what you choose. This is not a restaurant, you can't just order from the menu all the time. This is Kingdom, this is home. You eat what your mother cooked. You may even eat something that you don't like, but it is good for you. This is the instruction paradigm.

Have you ever been so impressed by someone, that you asked them to teach you how to do it? I have been impressed, but did I ask to be taught?

I heard a man talking about how he was able to borrow from himself. He read a book about being your own bank. So he borrowed from himself to pay for his daughter's college. I was impressed, but I didn't say, "Hey man, sit right down and teach me how to do that!"

Why not?

I like to think it was because I didn't want to make him spend that much time. Maybe it was because I didn't know him that well. But my suspicion is that the real cause was…Pride.

We don't like to admit what we don't know. We all want to seem informed. We all like to believe we are experts at everything. And since we have information literally at our fingertips, we are even more prideful. If I don't know, I can just research it myself. Pride can be a serious issue when we are talking about the flesh.

Paul outlines what you need to learn.

STEP 2: To put off the "Old Self" and put on the "New Self"

Ephesians 4:22-24
22 You were taught, with regard to your former way of life, to put off your old self, which is being corrupted by its deceitful desires; 23 to be made new in the attitude of your minds; 24 and to put on the new self, created to be like God in true righteousness and holiness.

At some point you have to make a break between who you were and who you are. The "old you" has to be put off. It doesn't just fall off. The old you has buttons and zippers, you have to actually take your old self off. You have to put childish ways behind you. It is like moving into a new house. When you get there, you are not interested in living with the previous owners. In the same way, when Christ moves in, He does not want to live with the old you that was running things. You have to put out the old man.

Then you have to put on the "new you." You have to be prepared for new thinking. You have to be prepared for a new attitude. You will have to examine the way that you have always thought and change your mind. This is literally what it means to repent. It means to go in a new direction, to turn from the way you were going, toward where you need to go.

It is time to see yourself as new. You have to be ready for change. You will never get a handle on your flesh if you stay around the same situations, the same environment, the same people, making the same choices, thinking the same thoughts. Put on the new you and get ready for a new life.

STEP 3 – Value HONESTY

Ephesians 4:25
25 Therefore each of you must put off falsehood and speak truthfully to your neighbor, for we are all members of one body.

Honesty is always going to be a key on this mountain of greatness. We have mentioned it before and here we are again, talking about being honest. Here the Word suggests that we be truthful with our neighbors. You have to put off falsehood. You have to stop being dishonest with people and that will help you to be honest with yourself.

We can all use a dose of this commendation, although always speaking the truth is challenging. My determination to be honest has caused me to speak less. If I don't have anything nice to say, I end up not saying anything at all. If I speak, I will have to say something that may sound nice and polite, but may not be totally true.

This is vitally important for a few reasons. First, you want people to be able to trust your word. You want to build a reputation of honesty and trustworthiness. You want to let your yes be yes and let your no be no.

Secondly and perhaps more importantly, the easier it is to lie to others, the easier it becomes to lie to yourself. If you are lying to yourself, then your flesh will win. This is how people end up evil. What they say to themselves is not the truth and it becomes easier and easier to allow the flesh to reign. Make honesty your policy. It is one of the best ways to keep the flesh under control.

STEP 4 - Be Angry but do not Sin

Ephesians 4:26-27
26 "In your anger do not sin"[d]: Do not let the sun go down while you are still angry," 27 and do not give the devil a foothold.

We addressed this at the beginning of this chapter. You can't be ruled by your emotions. At the same time, I love the clarity that the Word gives to us here. It is not the anger that is the sin. That is good news isn't it? For all of us who may wrestle with anger, it is good to know that the emotion itself is not the problem. It is your reaction to the emotion.

But for everyone who does deal with anger, the reaction is the main problem. Anger is something that feels good to hold onto. Of all the emotions, anger is the one that can elicit the strongest fleshly response. I can see exactly why the Word addresses anger. Holding on to that anger just perpetuates the fleshly response.

Paul's word is, don't let the sun go down on wrath. Don't go to bed angry. That is the wrong approach when keeping the flesh under control is the aim. Take a breath and let it go. Speak the truth in love, but let the anger leave. It robs you of the energy you need to maintain your position on the mountain.

When you hold on to the anger, you are making space for the enemy. The anger keeps the door open. You may make a mistake in anger one day, but when you hold on to the anger, you prolong the possibility of rash behavior.

Obviously since we are working on this fortress, we should know to keep the enemy out. Whatever you do, don't open the door for the enemy. You don't want to give him any access to you. You have to watch your doors.

When I was younger they used to recommend that you watch your "gates." You must keep an eye on the entry points – your eyes and your ears. Those are always the weak spots of any fortress. The enemy already has enough ammunition to throw at you. You don't want to help him by opening the door; don't help him destroy you.

STEP 5 - Be a Giver

Ephesians 4:28
28 *Anyone who has been stealing must steal no longer, but must work, doing something useful with their own hands, that they*

may have something to share with those in need.

You want to be generous. This keeps greed at bay and greed is a serious act of the flesh to keep your eye on. Greed is so insidious because we all have needs. We all need money, we all need food. And going after needs is a part of life.

The way to balance it out, is to be serious about generosity. You want to be the conduit of blessing for others. When you decide to give generously, you keep yourself from becoming overly focused on yourself. Selfishness is a serious act of the flesh. Giving of yourself maintains the balance that is needed.

This is why Jesus commanded that we serve each other. The one that wants to be great must be the servant of all. If you have been wise enough to accumulate wealth, you are great. You show that greatness by standing under the world, not over it. You become a leader in your community by supporting people less fortunate than you. Your generosity makes you great. No one great allows greed to control them

STEP 6 - Watch Your Mouth, Watch What You Say

Ephesians 4:29
29 Do not let any unwholesome talk come out of your mouths, but only what is helpful for building others up according to their needs, that it may benefit those who listen. 31 Get rid of all bitterness, rage and anger, brawling and slander, along with

every form of malice.

This passage is so simple that it barely needs an explanation. Your mouth and your flesh are connected, obviously. Your mouth is connected to so many of the issues that can trouble you when it comes to controlling the flesh. When Paul says, "who will save me from this body of death," he could have just as easily said, "who will save me from the words of my mouth?"

The ultimate challenge in the kingdom is to keep unwholesome talk from coming out of your mouth. When we think about sin, we have a tendency to focus on so many things other than these issues that can be connected to your mouth. But when we are talking about the flesh, your mouth is the key.

All of these potential issues are connected to your mouth:
- Bitterness is festered negativity. Negativity starts as a thought, but when you speak it, it can quickly turn into bitterness. Think about it, as you tell more and more people about what happened, soon bitterness takes hold.
- Rage and Brawling– the more you talk the angrier you can become. Have you ever started to tell someone about something that made you angry and you feel the anger returning? When you feel angry, you have to be careful about what you say. And if there is any way that anger can turn into physical violence, it is through what you say. Words almost always precede any physical altercation. What you say and what they say can lead to a fight.

- Slander – Slander is the evil you speak about other people. For some reason, our flesh loves gossip. We love to hear juicy stories about people and spread them. Most times we don't even check to see if the details are true, we just talk. I am determined, more than ever, not to feed my flesh the destruction of others.
- Malice – When love is the commandment, hatred is a serious enemy. Malice is when the hatred turns viscous. It is possible for your mind to actually cause you to plan evil. Petty and malicious actions are not the actions of someone that belongs on this greatness mountain.

7) Forgiveness

Ephesians 4:32
32 Be kind and compassionate to one another, forgiving each other, just as in Christ, God forgave you.

And finally, Paul says be kind, be nice, be compassionate. Treat other people the way you want to be treated. Judge the way you want to be judged. You examine yourself with compassion, examine others in the same way.

Forgiveness is a crucial factor in flesh control. Forgiveness is so big it almost needs its own wall in this fortress. You have to let people go. You have to walk in forgiveness. You even have to forgive your enemies. It doesn't make any sense to make all of this progress, only to be eaten from the inside by the cancer of un-forgiveness.

There are 2 types of Forgiveness:
A) Distant Forgiveness
B) Intimate Forgiveness

A) Distant Forgiveness is when you forgive someone, but you do not trust them again. I think this is why so many of us wrestle with forgiveness. We think that forgiveness means I have to be back at the same place I was with that person. Forgiving your ex does not mean that you have to get back with them. Distant forgiveness is not about the other person, it is about you.

You have to let them go so that you can reach the heights that are meant for you. You can't move on and hold on to them at the same time. Many of us are being held back by a person who isn't even thinking about us anymore.

Distant forgiveness does not require an apology; it does not require change. It does not even require any contact with the person. You let them go and move on.

B) Intimate Forgiveness is what you must practice in a close relationship. The person apologizes and you forgive them and move on. You have to be intentional about forgetting the issue. If you keep bringing it up, you have not really forgiven them.

And if you can't forgive, you won't be able to stay intimate with them.

Change and repentance is required for intimate forgiveness to work. You have to become new and then I will move forward with the new you, intimately. But if you stay the same and continue to violate me and hurt me in the same way, I will never be able to forget the thing that you did.

At that point, it isn't about forgetting, it is about change. Some people can't let things go, even when the person has seen the error and has decided to change. Some people don't believe in that change. If you are like that, understand, you will always wrestle with intimacy. No one is perfect, we all need forgiveness. Try to focus on how God forgives you and use that as fuel to forgive the people close to you.

How? Forgiveness is all about what you say next. So let me give you…

3 Phrases to say to help you forgive. In essence you are saying, "I forgive them because…

1) They don't know what they are doing
This is what Jesus says from the cross. **Luke 23:34**:
*Jesus said, "**Father, forgive them**, for they do not know what they are doing."*

You wash them in ignorance. They hurt me, but they didn't even know it. They did wrong, but they didn't know what they were doing.

2) They knew, but they meant well
We talked about this some in the "People Mountain" chapter. You have to know where people are coming from and what they intended. People who care, but still end up hurting you, they have to be forgiven.

This is the way that you treat adults from your past that did things to you "for your good" but you now realize that some of those things were over the line. You forgive, because they meant well.

3) They meant it for evil, but God has turned it
This is what Joseph said to his brothers. You meant to harm me, but God had other plans. This is one of the best things about the Lord. He is not the author of the evil, but He will take it and use it for your good. Joseph is #2 in Egypt. He went through difficulty, but look at how God turned it.

Look at you. They meant it for evil, but God can turn in. They tried to hurt you, but you have to forgive them. That forgiveness is the key to you walking in the blessing God has for you. Be determined not to let that pain define you. Let them go and walk in greatness.

The flesh is and will continue to be a battle for every believer. Until you leave this flesh, you will have to subdue it. In the same way that you have to wash your body and feed your body and exercise your body, you also have to control your body. The walls are spiritual, but you live in flesh. When you bring flesh into the fortress you will have to stay alert. You can do it. You can walk by faith and not by the flesh!

Chapter 9

The LAZINESS Wall

Matthew 9:37-38

37 Then Jesus said to his disciples, "The harvest is plentiful but the workers are few. 38 Ask the Lord of the harvest, therefore, to send out workers into his harvest field."

The Harvest requires work. You are here on the mountain of greatness and power. This is the time to start to walk in what God has promised. Are you ready? Are you ready to see some of the fruit of Canaan? I know that I am. But it is a mistake to think that this means that you can relax. This is not the time to take it easy.

Canaan is when the work really begins. God will be fighting for you and alongside you, but there is work to do. Nothing can pull you down off this mountain of greatness and opportunity, unless you get lazy.

Jesus makes an observation that we need to examine more closely. I know He is talking about souls; He is talking about people. But this concept applies to every aspect of harvest, especially when the harvest is plentiful. This was a phrase from biblical agricultural time. The larger the harvest, the bigger the work force required to take it in. Most people were able to manage with family and servants, but people who were wealthy ended up hiring workers during harvest time.

This point is so powerful. The greater the harvest, the greater the work. And Jesus is saying, "the problem isn't the harvest, the problem is the work."

Doesn't that bless you? You are worried about the results, you are concerned about the outcome. You wonder if there is enough money, is the market large enough, is your city big enough, is your gift powerful enough? I am here to tell you; the harvest is plentiful. Man, I am encouraging myself with this paragraph. The harvest is ripe, it is full, it is plentiful. It's not about the harvest; it is about the work.

Jesus says, "pray for workers." In other words, pray that God will send people to the kingdom, that are not lazy. Pray that God will send people to your company, that know how to work. Pray that God will give you a fire and a passion to get the work done.

I have hired many people. And when I am hiring someone, I am looking for someone with passion and energy. I don't always need someone who is experienced. Experience can be gained, experience can be taught – but not fire, you can't teach fire. It is hard to wash the laziness out of people.

This is the time for work. I tell young people all of the time, this is the time to get work done. You should fall asleep easy at night, so exhausted from the work you did that day. Youth should not be wasted "chillin." Youth provides you with an energy that you should use to secure your future.

And if you are not as young as you used to be, then you certainly have no time to waste. You have to be a worker; you have to stay busy. There is so much work to be done; there is so much harvest to be reaped. It's time to go to work.

Have you ever seen someone win one of those 2-minute shopping sprees? I have seen it on TV, someone running around in a store with a timer running and whatever they get in the cart within the time limit is theirs to keep. When the say go, the person takes off running and begins to fill that cart as quickly as they can.

Do you ever feel like you didn't work as hard as you should have when the harvest came? Have you ever wished you could get that harvest again? You know what you would do different this time. You wouldn't just work harder, you would work smarter. Well, can I prophesy to you through this book for a moment? Another harvest time is coming. It has to. Harvest time is seasonal.

Another harvest is coming and you need to be ready to do the work. Get your plans together to work smarter this time. There is always work to be done when you are in the kingdom. And there is always work to be done on this mountain of greatness and potential.

Let's spend a bit talking about the work. There are 5 types of work I want you ready to do...

1. Jesus Work

John 14:12
*"Very truly I tell you, whoever believes in me will do the **works** I have been doing and they will do even greater things than these, because I am going to the Father."*

We must do His work. We are the body of Christ; we are his body here in the earth. Jesus said that we would do even greater work because He is with the Father. By ascending He shows us that He has empowered us. And He now is able to live inside of us and do work through us.

The greatest Jesus work is to be like Jesus. That is the highest goal; that is the ultimate level to attain. Whenever I explain "Salvation," what is means to be saved, I describe it in this way.

There are 3 steps on the ladder of salvation.

Step 1 – Doing what the Word says to do.

I know this sounds basic, but there are many Christians who struggle just with obedience to the Word of God. If the Word says to forgive, there are no excuses; you forgive. We just spoke about forgiveness in the last chapter and I gave you a good reason to walk in forgiveness. But I shouldn't have to give anyone any reasons to forgive. You should forgive because the Word says to forgive.

Step 2 – Doing what Pleases the Lord

Ephesians 5:10 says, *"and find out what pleases the Lord."*

As much as we have to obey the Word, we have to be careful that we are not so caught up in the letter that we ignore the spirit of the law. You shouldn't use the Bible like it is some giant legal document and you are looking for loopholes in the document. You also have to do what pleases God.

Someone asked me, "Is it ok for me to go to this party at my job?" I said, "I don't know, you tell me."

People want pastors to absolve them of things that they know are wrong. I don't know what is going to happen at the party. I don't know what kind of party it is. I can assume that since it sounds like an office party, you should be there. But you have to know yourself. Do you do crazy things at office parties? Maybe you know something I don't know. And what's more, you are asking me because the Spirit is bothering you about this party.

Just because the bible does not specifically say, "thou shalt not go to office parties," does not mean the party is good for you. Paul says on two separate occasions in 1 Corinthians, that "not everything is beneficial." Something may be permissible, but that does not mean it will benefit you. You have to find out what pleases the Lord.

Step 3 – Doing what Jesus would do

That is the final level, to be like Jesus. It is daunting work. It is easy to say, "well, I'm not Jesus!"

What kind of husband would Jesus be? What kind of father would Jesus be? What kind of boss, what kind of employee would Jesus be? If I am just trying to do my best with Jesus by my side, there is room for me to make mistakes. I can excuse my behavior.

But when the aim is to be like Jesus, it ups the ante. Humility is never a problem when Jesus is the measuring line. Some people think that to be humble means to walk around low, quiet, not getting too much attention. But that is not humility. You can stand as tall as you want and be who you are. But when you stand next to Jesus and measure yourself against Jesus, you are put right back into your place.

2. Ground Work

Everyone has ground work to do.

A) You have to work on the soil that is you. You want to be good ground so that the Word can live in you. You have to break up the fallow ground in your own heart.

You should test the ground of your heart. What happens when you hear the Word? What happens when you read the Word? Do you believe it easily? Does it take root in you? We are talking about you and your fortress on the mountain of greatness. You can't stay there on my understanding of the Word. Even now, I am sharing my understanding with you, so that it can become your understanding. But in all you do, you have to get an understanding.

B) You have to lay the foundation for the future. You are a builder. You have to build upon the rock that is Christ. You have to be careful about your "first works." That is why we took you step by step through the mountains. We needed to lay that foundation so that you could be everything that God desires for you to be. Greatness doesn't happen overnight. Greatness is developed over time. Greatness begins with the right foundation.

Have you ever seen a house that is starting to lean? We have so many codes and inspections today that we rarely see this anymore. But I remember seeing some homes like this in Virginia when I used to visit my great grandmother. There is nothing scarier than a home that wasn't built right. It doesn't matter how you try to paint it or dress it up. It doesn't matter what kind of furniture you put in the house. If the house is not built on the right foundation, then there will be problems later on.

3. Word Work

We have work to do when it comes to the Word. There is the consistency of study, devotional time in the Word. This is so important.

In Matthew 7:24, Jesus said: **24** "Therefore everyone who hears these words of mine and puts them into practice is like a wise man who built his house on the rock. **25** The rain came down, the streams rose, and the winds blew and beat against that house; yet it did not fall, because it had its foundation on the rock

We have to…

A) Hear the Word

You have to keep your ears open to the Word. You have to keep hearing the Logos – the written word and you have to keep hearing the Rhema – the spoken word. Bear in mind, the Logos and the Rhema will always agree. God will never speak a word to you that does not agree with what He has already said in His Word.

B) Practice the Word

The Word doesn't work if you don't obey it. Your biggest prayer to God should be for Him to help you to be obedient. So many problems would be avoided if we could just practice what the Word says.

Putting the Word into practice implies that the recommendations of the Word become a habit for you. I don't know if you have any bad habits, but many people have issues with bad habits. Bad habits are rarely intentionally formed. In order to override a bad habit, you need to form a good habit. If you can complete a task for 21 days straight, you will form a habit.

You want to practice the Word and make the Word your usual practice. The next time you get angry, practice what the Word says to do. That is work, but it is good work to do. Soon that will become your normal practice.

4. Faith Work

Jesus was asked a question in… John 6:28-29

28 Then they asked him,"What must we do to do the works God requires?" 29 Jesus answered, "The work of God is this: to believe in the one he has sent."

What is the work that God requires? Faith, belief and trusting in God; you have to continually walk after something you don't yet see. This whole book is on faith, so you are doing that work.

You have to keep your faith built up. You have to stay in "faith shape." You never know when a fight might break out. You have to keep your weapons close by. Faith is work; faith is not easy. But it is fulfilling work; it is work that can move mountains!

5. Church Work

Although we live in a world where everyone wants to personalize everything, remember that community is important. There is something powerful about connection with other believers – it feeds your faith. Although Hebrew 10 admonishes us to stay faithful to church, we are now living in a time when people want to view church online. We want to personalize the church moment to suit us.

And as much as I love the convenience of that, a significant part of church life is the opportunity to serve. You don't just attend church to get, you attend church to give. As Jesus said, "it is more blessed to give then to receive." You have to be more than a consumer to really walk in kingdom power. You have to be a producer.

It is a point that I have been determined to make in this book and I trust I have not failed. This "mountain moving power" is given to people that ultimately will use it for more than just themselves. If you want to be a winner, then join the winning team.

I trust that you are not just reading this book in the spiritual vacuum of your own theological thinking. It is wonderful that the Word is alive and that it speaks to everyone. But that does not mean that you do not need the church. You need to hear a Word from God. For you to stay on this mountain, you need to do the work of consistency at church.

When I say "Church Work" I mean 2 things...
- A. Serving in the local church
- B. Serving the Kingdom outside of church

A) Serving in the Local Church
It is important to be faithful to church. We have to keep in mind that Jesus came to do 2 things, to destroy the work of the devil and to establish His church. He said to his disciples that He would build His church. It is important for people to be able to go to a place where God is praised and the Word is preached. It is important, in a world that is growing more and more unspiritual, for there to be a place where matters of the spirit are emphasized.

The church does not work without people. I have read the statistics that the younger generation does not want to go to church, but that has to be a trend that we fight. We cannot accept that as the new norm. People need the church; the world needs the church.

The local church needs people – your local church needs you. Please don't let a leader, or a rude usher, or something petty to cause you to turn your back on church. As a Pastor, can I just speak for all the pastors out there? We need you.

We need you to…

Volunteer – the volunteer staff is the life blood of the church. The church cannot pay for all the people it takes for the church to function. We need children's ministry workers, parking team, ushers, greeters, singers, media team workers, maintenance team workers. We need faithful consistent workers.

Give – the church needs faithful givers, people who tithe, people who give offerings. The church needs people who will give to special projects so that the church will live beyond them. If you want to be blessed on the mountain, you have to pay your tithes.

God said He would rebuke the devourer on your behalf when you tithe. If you are wrestling with the devourer right now, perhaps your giving is the issue. The enemy never comes into power because he is strong. The enemy comes into power because there is idolatry among the people of God.

Might I suggest, we have not lost the control because unbelievers have grown in power. We have lost control because we worship other gods. n biblical times it was Baal, in modern times it is money. You can't serve both God and money.

Be Faithful – we need you to come consistently. I read a statistic that said the average church attender comes to church twice a month. What happened to keeping a Sabbath day holy? What happened to faithfulness and consistency? I asked my church once, "what kind of church do you think we would have if you weren't sure when I was coming? Would you invite someone if you were thinking, 'man, I sure hope Pastor Andy comes today!' What kind of church would we have?"

In the same way, what kind of church will we have if we cannot depend on you to be faithful? For everyone reading this book, I trust you are faithful to church. I don't know how many mountains you are going to move sitting at home on a Sunday.

B) Serving the Kingdom Outside of the Church

The church has to extend outside of the 4 walls. We have to touch the community. We have to touch the world. You have to find your place in the body. What are you called to do for God besides just serve in the church? I know we spent a chapter on "Purpose." You have to know your purpose for being on the planet. You also have to know your purpose for being in the kingdom. Perhaps you have come to the kingdom for just such a time as this. What is your calling? In case you did not know this, everyone is called.

To help you find your calling, let me give you some clear-cut roles that you may be gifted to fill. When I talk about serving the kingdom, I mean…

1) Evangelism – winning souls for Christ, telling people about what God has done for you. You don't have to be a biblical scholar to tell your testimony. God has done something great in your life. We don't need to hear that testimony in church; we need people in the world to hear it.

There was a time when everyone was taught to witness. Remember that, did you go to church during that time? People used to go around with tracts, the 4 spiritual laws, ways to minister Christ to people. What happened to that? Are we too afraid to offend people? People need the Lord.

We may laugh at the Mormon missionaries riding or walking around in their black pants and white shirts, but Mormonism is one the fastest growing religions in the world today. We who have the truth, we have to get back to this. And for some of you, this is your calling. If you work in sales, if your love talking to people, if you can talk an Eskimo into buying an ice maker, we need you to share Christ with someone. The Word says, "he/she that wins souls is wise."

2) Missions – showing the love of God with no strings attached. To represent the love of God to a people who may not know who Jesus is, this is a powerful calling. To touch the less fortunate, to bring them the love of Christ by caring for their physical needs, is work that needs to be done.

Human need is the gateway for people to come into contact with the master of needs. God is the provider, the master of needs. When you dig a well or provide medicine; when you provide a meal and educate a child, you are reaching outside of the church and touching the world. When you are great, your reach is extended.

3) Living – letting your light shine, is something that we need in the kingdom today. We have so many talkers, but not enough walkers. Anyone can talk a good game, but can you play. Anyone can go to church and smile and be nice and fake, but can you practice what you preach.

When you step outside of the church, that is when kingdom work begins. When we pray, "thy kingdom come, thy will be done," we are actually praying about the actions of people. We have to keep that in mind. When we ask God to move, we are asking Him to move over the hearts of people. When we ask God to bless, we are asking Him to touch the generosity inside of people and cause them to give. When we pray for the country, we are asking God to affect the way that leaders act and the decisions that they will make.

The actions of people, that is what all of this is about. For you to have faith that God can touch others, He has to be able to touch you. This is the foundational idea behind the "beam in your own eye" concept. How can you believe that God will touch someone else to give, if He cannot touch you and cause you to give? How can you ask God to touch your teenagers heart and cause him to be careful, if God has not been able to get you to see the wisdom of caution?

Something happened to us in the body of Christ. We became so focused on winning the world, that we forgot the other vital role of the believer. We have to let our lights shine so that men will see how we live and give God glory.

We became focused on the world agreeing with us that Jesus was Lord. When they didn't agree, we judged them as wrong. They are wrong, but then we took another step. Because they were wrong, we stopped caring about their opinion of us. We stopped caring if the respected us or not. But we have to understand, agreement begins with respect.

I would never agree with someone that I didn't respect. Even if they made a good point or said something seemingly intelligent, that would not cause me to agree with them. No matter what

Hitler said, we would never agree with him. No matter what Jeffrey Dahmer said, we would never agree, because we have no respect for him.

There was a time when the word "Christian" meant that you were respectful and chaste and disciplined. When someone described you as a good "Christian man," a "God-fearing woman," it meant that you were careful about how you lived. It didn't just mean that you were looking to be blessed.

I love the idea of prosperity. This book is about making it to great. Right now we are talking about staying on the mountain of greatness. But we can't exchange moral integrity for wealth and blessing. We have to chase both. I believe the church needs a makeover. Have you seen any of those makeover shows? My wife loves the home makeover programs. She loves the reveal at the end, when the house is renovated.

We need a renovation and then a reveal. The house of God needs someone to come in and do a remodel on us. And we need to begin like Jesus and ask, "who do men say that we are?" What is the prevailing opinion about the church?

We have to be prepared for the answer that will come. Some of the assumptions will be wrong, but some will be based on how we are, who we are and how we carry ourselves. It is time for us to do the tough work again. It is time for us to be great, not just ask God for great things. We can't ask God to give us greatness and not ask Him to make us internally great.

There is still so much work to be done. I know that it can be tough. You can see the finish line, but it is miles away. One of the challenges of having a great vision, is that the larger it is, the easier it is to see from a great distance. Just because you saw it 10 years ago did not mean that it was going to happen right away. Actually, you had to keep walking to get to this point.

Ok, now you are here and you are wondering, "do I have enough energy to make it the rest of the way?" YOU DO! YOU CAN DO THE WORK!!! Get busy, victory is in your hands. You have come too far to turn back now. God will renew your strength. He will give you the endurance to make it to the end!

Chapter 10

The TIME Wall

Ephesians 5:15-16
15 *Be very careful, then, how you live—not as unwise but as wise,* **16** *Redeeming the time, because the days are evil.*

We are now ready to build the final wall on our fortress. This wall stands for "Time." God lives outside of time. He knows the end from the beginning. When we leave this world, we will begin to walk with God in eternity. But until then, time is a factor that we have to wrestle with. You can't make the clock slow down. You can eat right and exercise, but you still have a limited number of days to be on this planet.

You can't think about faith and destiny and greatness, without thinking about time. We have to be prepared for what time will require of us. We have to learn to wait on God, but at the same time, we don't have time to waste. It is a discussion we need to have and I believe an excellent way for us to end this book.

Do you ever think to yourself how reckless you were when you were younger? Can you remember a time when you should have died? You were so crazy and looking back on it now, you realize how closely you slipped past death?

The next street over from the street I grew up on, was a steep hill. I used to love to ride my bike down the hill as fast as I could. The bottom of the hill emptied right into my street. I don't know how I am alive today. I never slowed down, I just shot across the street without looking.

Maturity makes you careful. Hopefully you have gained some wisdom by now. You got some sense before it was too late, and now, like the Word says, you are "very careful" how you live, not as unwise, but as wise.

When you get careful, you start to think about time. Time is one of the things that we all share in common. Time is the most valuable commodity in the world. Time is the one thing that you cannot get back. When wisdom comes upon you and you reach for destiny, time becomes a factor. You start to count your days and you start to think about all the time you wasted. Then, you begin to pray, "Lord, don't let it be too late."

Anybody wish you had a time machine? What would you do if you could back and talk to yourself when you were 16? What would you tell your 30-year-old self? What if you could just go back 2 years? If I could just go back 5 years, 10 years, everything would be different. These thoughts make you start to...

Redeem the Time

The (NIV) says, "making the most of every opportunity," you want to knock on every door. You want to make the most of the time you have remaining. I realize that I don't have time to waste. Time starts to fly as you get older. You will be on your way to heaven before you know it.

You become aware of each moment. You start to look at the clock. When you are a child you don't own a watch. When you mature, you become aware of the time. You realize that you need to know what season you are in.

There are 2 types of faith:

1) Instant Action Faith - Instant action faith is the kind of faith that we all love. We want something to happen right away. We love the miracles that happen in that same hour. We love "overnight" results. We love to hear stories where someone prayed and something happened instantly. We love those testimonies.

I definitely believe in that. I believe that God can turn it around in a moment. If you are wondering if it is too late, more often than not, the answer is that it is not too late. Not with God involved, not with the Lord on your side. Abraham had a child at 100 years old. Anything is possible with God! At the same time, I have come to realize that we have to learn to use the second type of faith. And that is:

2) Persistent Consistent Faith - I think of it as "farmer faith." This faith to me is "Faith for the overflow." The thing about overflow, is that overflow takes patience, overflow takes time. However, if you can't wait, you may sell out "great" for "ok, but right now."

Let me give you an example. Let's say that you want a lot of acorns. If you want more than enough acorns, you can have that right now. You could go to the seed store and buy a box of acorns. There would be thousands of acorns in that box. You would have more than enough and you would have them quickly. But that is not overflow. Overflow requires "Farmer faith." You take that acorn, you plant it, you fertilize it and you water it. After many years, that acorn becomes an oak tree. And when that oak tree becomes mature, you will have so many acorns you will be giving them away. You will never buy acorns again. You will be stepping on them, they will be crunching under your feet. You will have thousands of acorns for hundreds of years.

A huge part of the faith walk is knowing when to use which type of faith, in which moment. To some extent, that has been the basic premise of this book. When we think about "moving a mountain," we primarily think "instant action faith." You speak to the mountain and it moves into the sea.

As we dug deeper, we began to acknowledge that not all mountains move that quickly. Being unaware of that is not your fault. I don't know if you have ever heard this from any other faith preacher. But I am here to tell you, you are going to have to take a look at each mountain. You are going to have to become familiar with each mountain. The faith needed may be "farmer faith," or, it may be "persistent consistent faith" that moves the mountain.

In other words, you may have to learn to wait.

I know, I just swore. Forgive me. The word "wait" is not a word any of us really like to hear. The only reason we wait is because we have to wait. If I did a conference on *waiting,* no one would show up. We don't want to hear anyone talk about waiting, we want every preacher to tell us to, "give God a RIGHT NOW SHOUT! God is about to do something for you RIGHT NOW! Shout YES SOMEBODY!"

We love the phrase, "Right NOW!" But if we are honest, we will admit, things take time. Waiting can be brutal, especially if you have no understanding. So, for all of us who are waiting and determined to be of good courage, allow me to help.

What makes the wait unbearable is, not knowing what time it is. When you can look at your watch and count down the hours, the wait is still a wait, but it's not as tough. For you to be patient, for you to deal with time, you have to know your season.

So, let's finish up by talking about times and seasons on this mountain of great. It is not always spring on this mountain. While I am writing, it is winter. It is cold outside; it snowed the other day. After a while, you can get tired of the snow and the cold. But it will be ok, because winter is a season. You are not about to die, this is only a season. This is not the end, it is only a season. You don't need to get rid of all of your summer clothes. It won't be cold forever, this is a season, it will pass.

One of the most famous passages in the bible, Ecclesiastes 3, addresses the inescapable reality of times and seasons. Through His Word, God sets a very clear moment for us to identify. He wants to help us not to panic when things are not happening when we want them to. He wants to give us the tools to have the patience required to walk with Him. He is the author of life and He knows what we go through. Fortunately, He has given us the answer in His Word.

When I look at Ecclesiastes 3, I see 7 seasons. Let's think of them as 7 months in the "Power/Miracle Calendar.

Let's start by looking at the passage…

Ecclesiastes 3:1-8
1 There is a time for everything,
  and a season for every activity under the heavens:
2 a time to be born and a time to die,
  a time to plant and a time to uproot,
3 a time to kill and a time to heal,
  a time to tear down and a time to build,
4 a time to weep and a time to laugh,
  a time to mourn and a time to dance,
5 a time to scatter stones and a time to gather them,
  a time to embrace and a time to refrain from embracing,
6 a time to search and a time to give up,
  a time to keep and a time to throw away,
7 a time to tear and a time to mend,
  a time to be silent and a time to speak,
8 a time to love and a time to hate,
  a time for war and a time for peace.

Here are the 7 seasons I see:

1. NEW - *Time for Something New*

There is a time to be born and a time to plant; a time to make that beginning. You may not see fruit immediately because the thing is new. Your relationship is new. Your marriage is new. You are not going to be in year 1, where you will be in year 20. You have to be patient.

The business is new; the church is new. People will come, you will see a harvest, but this is the beginning time. People are in a rush these days, they don't want to spend the time it takes in newness.

Before you give up, give it a bit more time. This may be the planting time. There is a time to plant.

We also have to be aware of when it is time to start. It is possible to miss your window. Some beginnings are time sensitive. You have to make the most of your time. It is possible to be too late. So, you have to be careful not to miss your season. You have to find your purpose as quickly as possible, because you can miss planting time.

If you are 7 feet tall, but 43 years old, it is too late to play in the NBA. We could make an argument that God made you 7 feet tall to take advantage of a fun way to become rich. But if you are 43, it is too late.

I know we don't like to think about this, but it is reality. There are some areas where it is never too late and then there are areas where it is too late. If you are a 63-year-old woman, it is too late to have kids. If your purpose was to be a mother, then you are going to have to be a spiritual mother. It is a reality. God can turn back the clock and He did, for Abraham and Sarah, but it was so rare that even they couldn't believe it. Sarah laughed.

I am not trying to discourage you, I am trying to tell you the truth. There is a time to get things done and there is a planting time. Despise not the humble beginning. You will reap a harvest if you don't give up.

2. STOP - Time to Stop

There is a time to die, a time to uproot and a time to tear down. Knowing when to quit is a priceless wisdom. You need to know how to be patient, but you also need to know when it is time to give in. Everything you try is not going to work. Have you failed at anything yet? I have. I found out that it was something that God did not want me doing. I wish I could have heard from him directly. It's possible that He was trying to tell me, but I just didn't listen. So, the way I found out was that I failed.

But how do you know when it is time to stop? I was listening to a lecture by a successful CEO. He said that there were 2 keys to being successful in business. The first thing is the ability to see what is coming next. The reason we don't see Blockbuster video anymore is because the video world changed to streaming, and Blockbuster lost to Netflix.

The second thing is the ability to know what to stop doing so that you can do the new thing. You can't do everything. How long are you going to manufacture VHS tapes after DVDs have arrived? At some point you can't afford to do both. You have to know when to stop.

I am constantly looking for God to confirm His Word with signs following. If the Lord wants you to do something, you will know. People love to cosign God's name to things. But the bible says in Romans 3:4, *"Let God be true, though it makes every man a liar."* You may have to admit that you were mistaken. But I have found that this is very difficult for Christians to do. I have lost relationships with people because I dared to tell them that it was time to stop.

Believe me, if God is behind it, fire will fall. If fire does not fall, _____, you fill in the blank!

3. FOCUS - Time to be Serious
The world says there is a time to weep, a time to mourn. Ecclesiastes 7:2 takes it even farther when it says, *2 It is better to go to a house of mourning than to go to a house of feasting for death is the destiny of everyone; the living should take this to heart.*

There are moments to be serious. When you go to a funeral, it causes you to come to grips with mortality. You begin to see time in a clearer way. I just buried one of my charter members, he was 2 days older than me. When people in your generation start to die, it makes you focus.

I know some people avoid funerals. "They are too sad," is what people say. But that sadness can make you see.

We wrote a whole chapter on work, on fighting laziness and complacency. When you are hard at work at a task, it can cause you to be serious. You seem upset, but it is not that you are angry, you are just focused. Gathering stones is hard work. Scattering stones is heavy hard work. You can whistle while you work, but you have to get the work done. Life is not always a party.

There are times that can just be tough. I think I mentioned the fact that my wife and I have triplets. When they were first born, it was a tough time. Imagine 3 infants, we had to keep a schedule on the wall to keep track of the feedings and diaper changes. It was crazy. They wouldn't stay asleep at first because we had them in separate cribs but they were used to being near each other. We finally put them all in a bed together. But there was always something else.

It was like that until they were about…actually it is still tough. Now they are 18, and they are driving. They are starting to date and trying to eat everything they see. I have to write my name on my food and they still eat it. When they were 6 months old, if you had asked me if I was happy in my marriage, that wouldn't have been a fair question.

I was happy that I had 3 sons, but my wife was so busy, we never got any time together. When she came to bed, she was exhausted. We got through it, but it was a tough season. We got made it through because we knew it was just a season. We stayed encouraged by imagining when they went to school for the first time. She cried when our daughter went to school for the first time, but not the boys. That was a day of celebration. We had made it through a tough season.

You can't expect laughter and happiness and joy every second. If you have lost someone close to you, this is a sad time. There is nothing wrong with being sad during the sad seasons. Those seasons come, but they only linger if you do not make your way through that season. Your weeping may endure for the night, but joy is coming in the morning. You just have to last until morning.

4. LAUGH - Time to have Fun

There is a time for joy and laughter. The joy balances out the pain. I have experienced a joy that was so complete that it erased the memory of the pain I endured. It is like when a woman has a child. After 26 hours in labor, you don't name the child, "This Hurts Thompson," you name them something wonderful like Kayla. Why? Because the moment you saw Kayla's little face, the joy of holding her in your arms erased the pain to get her here.

That is why laughter and joy are required for life. You can't be serious all of the time. Some of us were raised so strict holiness that you almost felt guilty for having too much fun. Since sin was fun…Um…Can we admit that? Sin was fun for the moment, but the consequences were not worth it. If Eve had bitten the fruit and it tasted like feces, she never would have given some to Adam to try. Sin was fun, but the wages of that sin was death. OK, so, since sin was fun, we can begin to equate all fun with sin. But it is possible to have a good time and not be in a holy ghost meeting every second. Church is wonderful, but I don't want to be there all day. There is a time to worship in church and then there is a time to go to the movies and eat popcorn and junior mints and mini-snickers and enjoy a show.

That leads me to the next season…

5. Rest – a Time to Vacation

There is a time to heal, a time to mend and a time to rebuild your reserves. Jesus gave us one day in seven to rest. The Sabbath is supposed to be a day when you do no work. There is a time to work and then there is a time to relax and chill. There is a time to focus and then there is a time to get away and let your hair down. It is possible to get so caught up in your work, that you don't take the time to recuperate and rest. And sometimes, God has to make you rest. He makes me lie down in green pastures. Whenever I get sick, I know that it is the germ and that I need rest. When you are running for Jesus, you can forget to stop and sleep. When you have goals, when greatness and power is your goal, it can be all consuming. You have to know when to take a break.

Sabbath is a holy time. The same God who created church and worship, also created the beach. When you are laying there getting tan and feeling the wind caress you, you are being touched by God's power.

6. LOVE - Time to Feel the Love

There is a time to embrace and there is a time to love. There is a time to search for meaningful relationships. It is possible to be so focused on your work, or so focused on your educational goals, that you can miss your window to build lasting connections.
I am so grateful that I found my wife when I did. Or should I say that she found me since she basically stalked me, since I am so abundantly wonderful. By the way, if you believe that I also have a bridge to sell you in NY! But I digress...

She loved me before I became this "Pastor Andy" person. She loved me before I became this international best-selling author of this book entitled, "MORE – Accepting Mountains as the Path to Greatness." It would be difficult to find love after success. You're not quite sure who to trust. Do people love you for who you are, or for what you can do for them?

Fellowship and connection is so important. You have to unite with others. Jesus spent 3 years with His disciples. During that time, he was ministering to the world, but he was also building his team.

You may not be winning, but if you are building your team, you are still ahead of the game. Finding love is finding life. Putting a priority on unity can help you to be silent. There is a time to speak, but there is also a time to say nothing. I don't just hold my peace for God to fight my battles, I also hold my peace to maintain the unity that I need with my partners. Everything doesn't need to be said.

7. WAR - Time for Separation

There is a time for war, a time to hate and a time to throw away. There is a time to gather and then there is a time to stow away and be separate. You won't always be popular.

It is wonderful to be popular; it is wonderful when everyone loves you. But can you function when that is not the case? Jesus had power when they were yelling, "Hosanna!" And He still had power when they yelled, "Crucify Him!"

I have a revelation for you. Ready? Not everyone is going to like you.
Sometimes success will cause a break from certain people.
When you stand up, you stand out. And when you stand out, you can attract enemies. You have to know when it is time to fight. It is not always peace time.

When I was a kid, we used to play a card game called "War." Did you play that game? There came a time in the game where you said, "I Declare War!" You have to know when to say that.

When the enemy comes in like a flood, "I Declare WAR!" There is an attack against my physical body, "I Declare WAR!" You are on the mountain and you see the enemy determined to knock you off. But you know that this is your moment. This is your season. And often times, the only way to peace is through a battle. War time is never fun. You get hit and you get hurt, but you press on. The weapons are formed but they will not prosper. And with God on your side, you know that even if you lose a battle, you will still win the war.

Psalm 1:1-3 says,*1 Blessed is the one who does not walk in step with the wicked or stand in the way that sinners take or sit in the company of mockers, 2 but whose delight is in the law of the Lord, and who meditates on his law day and night. 3 That person is like a tree planted by streams of water, which yields its fruit in season and whose leaf does not wither— whatever they do prospers.*

Look at verse 3.
The second line says, "which yields its fruit in season." I know we want to be fruitful all the time, but fruitfulness is seasonal. If you are not seeing the results right now, you have to look at the time. If you are cold, look at the season. Know where you are and WHEN you are there and you will find peace on the mountain.

The problem is not you, it is not God it and it's not even the Enemy. You are moving from one season to another season.

Keep that farmer faith going. Wait on the Lord, be of good courage and He will strengthen your heart. Wait I say on the Lord!

Conclusion

Love the Ride…

One of the biggest mistakes that we can make as people of faith is to be more in love with the destination than the journey. It is like being on a cruise. The ports are great, but the time on the ship is also what you paid for. You didn't just pay to get to the Bahamas, you paid to enjoy the time it took to get there.

We have to apply this attitude to our miracle. The greatest miracles are the journeys that you find yourself on. It is like being on a roller coaster. My boys talk me into it every time we are in an amusement park. As we slowly ascend, I am thinking, "what am I doing on this ride? How did I let these boys talk me into this? I am too old for this!"

I start looking at the steps that lead back down and wonder if there is any way I can get them to stop the ride and just let me walk down. Then, when you get to the top, they ruthlessly let you dangle for a moment…and then that first drop. The best thing to do is just throw your hands up and yell. There isn't anything else to do.

When the ride is over and your heart is racing and exhilaration has made your eyes water, you realize that this is why you came to the park. You came to get the bejeezus scared out of you, and live to tell it. You came for the ride.

That, my friend, is faith. Faith is a journey; faith is a ride. It can be a scary ride and sometimes you want to get off, but that would be a mistake. This is what you were made for; this is what life is supposed to be about. You don't want to sit on the bench and hold everyone's coats and bags and hats and watch them ride. You want to get in line, let that bar come down over your shoulders, feel your feet dangle, and wonder, "will I survive this?"

You will. You are here to win. You are here for MORE!!! You are here to feel the thrill of victory, snatched out of the jaws of defeat. You are God's child. This is what you were made for. You'll conquer each mountain and fall in love with mountains.

Fall in love with giants. Fall in love with the challenge. Do the tough thing, do the hard thing. Choose the path less chosen. Walk on the water. Don't just cheer for Peter, dare to get out and walk. Believe in God, believe in His power and believe in His calling. Believe in your destiny. Believe in yourself.

With all this faith, with all that we now believe, these mountains have no choice—they MUST move and MORE is CERTAIN!

CPSIA information can be obtained
at www.ICGtesting.com
Printed in the USA
FSHW021025220919